NATURAL LANGUAGE AND COMPUTATIONAL LINGUISTICS
An Introduction

ELLIS HORWOOD SERIES IN COMPUTERS AND THEIR APPLICATIONS
Series Editor: IAN CHIVERS, Senior Analyst, The Computer Centre, King's College, London, and formerly Senior Programmer and Analyst, Imperial College of Science and Technology, University of London

Abramsky, S. & Hankin, C.J.	ABSTRACT INTERPRETATION OF DECLARATIVE LANGUAGES
Alexander, H.	FORMALLY-BASED TOOLS AND TECHNIQUES FOR HUMAN–COMPUTER DIALOGUES
Atherton, R.	STRUCTURED PROGRAMMING WITH BBC BASIC
Atherton, R.	STRUCTURED PROGRAMMING WITH COMAL
Baeza-Yates, R.A.	TEXT SEARCHING ALGORITHMS
Bailey, R.	FUNCTIONAL PROGRAMMING WITH HOPE
Barrett, R., Ramsay, A. & Sloman, A.	POP-11
Beardon, C., Lumsden, D. & Holmes, G.	NATURAL LANGUAGE AND COMPUTATIONAL LINGUISTICS: An Introduction
Berztiss, A.	PROGRAMMING WITH GENERATORS
Bharath, R.	COMPUTERS AND GRAPH THEORY: Representing Knowledge for Processing by Computers
Bishop, P.	FIFTH GENERATION COMPUTERS
Bullinger, H.-J. & Gunzenhauser, H.	SOFTWARE ERGONOMICS
Burns, A.	NEW INFORMATION TECHNOLOGY
Carberry, J.C.	COBOL
Carlini, U. & Villano, U.	TRANSPUTERS AND PARALLEL ARCHITECTURES
Chivers, I.D.	AN INTRODUCTION TO STANDARD PASCAL
Chivers, I.D.	MODULA 2
Chivers, I.D. & Sleighthome, J.	INTERACTIVE FORTRAN 77
Clark, M.W.	PC-PORTABLE FORTRAN
Clark, M.W.	TEX
Cockshott, W. P.	A COMPILER WRITER'S TOOLBOX: How to Implement Interactive Compilers for PCs with Turbo Pascal
Cockshott, W. P.	PS-ALGOL IMPLEMENTATIONS: Applications in Persistent Object-Oriented Programming
Colomb, R.	IMPLEMENTING PERSISTENT PROLOG
Cope, T.	COMPUTING USING BASIC
Curth, M.A. & Edelmann, H.	APL
Dahlstrand, I.	SOFTWARE PORTABILITY AND STANDARDS
Dandamudi, S. P.	HIERARCHICAL HYPERCUBE MULTICOMPUTER INTERCONNECTION NETWORKS
Dongarra, J., Duff, I., Gaffney, P., & McKee, S.	VECTOR AND PARALLEL COMPUTING
Dunne, P.E.	COMPUTABILITY THEORY: Concepts and Applications
Eastlake, J.J.	A STRUCTURED APPROACH TO COMPUTER STRATEGY
Eisenbach, S.	FUNCTIONAL PROGRAMMING
Ellis, D.	MEDICAL COMPUTING AND APPLICATIONS
Ennals, J.R.	ARTIFICIAL INTELLIGENCE
Ennals, J.R.	BEGINNING MICRO-PROLOG
Ennals, J.R., *et al.*	INFORMATION TECHNOLOGY AND EDUCATION
Filipič, B.	PROLOG USER'S HANDBOOK
Ford, N.	COMPUTER PROGRAMMING LANGUAGES
Ford, N.J., Ford, J.M., Holman, D.F. & Woodroffe, M.R.	COMPUTERS AND COMPUTER APPLICATIONS: An Introduction for the 1990s
Grill, E.	RELATIONAL DATABASES
Grune, D. & Jacobs, C.J.H.	PARSING TECHNIQUES: A Practical Guide
Guariso, G. & Werthner, H.	ENVIRONMENTAL DECISION SUPPORT SYSTEMS
Harland, D.M.	CONCURRENCY AND PROGRAMMING LANGUAGES
Harland, D.M.	POLYMORPHIC PROGRAMMING LANGUAGES
Harland, D.M.	REKURSIV
Harris, D.J.	DEVELOPING DEDICATED DBASE SYSTEMS
Henshall, J. & Shaw, S.	OSI EXPLAINED, 2nd Edition
Hepburn, P.H.	FURTHER PROGRAMMING IN PROLOG
Hepburn, P.H.	PROGRAMMING IN MICRO-PROLOG MADE SIMPLE
Hill, I.D. & Meek, B.L.	PROGRAMMING LANGUAGE STANDARDISATION
Hirschheim, R., Smithson, S. & Whitehouse, D.	MICROCOMPUTERS AND THE HUMANITIES: Survey and Recommendations
Hutchins, W.J.	MACHINE TRANSLATION
Hutchison, D.	FUNDAMENTALS OF COMPUTER LOGIC
Hutchison, D. & Silvester, P.	COMPUTER LOGIC
Koopman, P.	STACK COMPUTERS
Koops, A. & J. Dreijklufft	WORKING WITH COREL DRAW!
Kenning, M.-M. & Kenning, M.J.	COMPUTERS AND LANGUAGE LEARNING: Current Theory and Practice
Koskimies, K. & Paaki, J.	AUTOMATING LANGUAGE IMPLEMENTATION
Koster, C.H.A.	TOP-DOWN PROGRAMMING WITH ELAN
Last, R.	ARTIFICIAL INTELLIGENCE TECHNIQUES IN LANGUAGE LEARNING
Lester, C.	A PRACTICAL APPROACH TO DATA STRUCTURES

NATURAL LANGUAGE AND COMPUTATIONAL LINGUISTICS
An Introduction

COLIN BEARDON   B.A., M.Sc., Ph.D., M.A.
Rediffusion Simulation Centre, Brighton Polytechnic
DAVID LUMSDEN   B.A., M.A., Ph.D.
GEOFF HOLMES   B.Sc., Ph.D.
both of the University of Waikato, New Zealand

ELLIS HORWOOD
NEW YORK   LONDON   TORONTO   SYDNEY   TOKYO   SINGAPORE

First published in 1991 by
ELLIS HORWOOD LIMITED
Market Cross House, Cooper Street,
Chichester, West Sussex, PO19 1EB, England

A division of
Simon & Schuster International Group
A Paramount Communications Company

Printed and bound in Great Britain
by Redwood Press Limited, Melksham, Wiltshire

British Library Cataloguing in Publication Data

Natural language and computational linguistics: an introduction
Colin Beardon, David Lumsden, Geoff Holmes
CIP catalogue record for this book is available from the British Library

ISBN 0–13–612813–0

Library of Congress Cataloging-in-Publication Data available

Contents

Chapter 7 - Text Generation

1

Introduction

1.1 Artificial and natural language

When we say that a language is natural, as opposed to artificial or formal, we are saying that it is something that already exists and fulfills various functions in our dealings with other people. We use natural language primarily to communicate with other people and it has evolved to enable us to say all sorts of things in all sorts of situations. An artificial language, by contrast, is something we prescribe. It normally has a specific purpose and is far more restrictive in the things that you can use it for. A good example of an artificial language is one of the various programming languages that have been designed to make the task of programming easier (e.g. BASIC, Pascal, COBOL). The programming language COBOL, for example, was intended to be English-like but you would have a lot of difficulty trying to write a letter to someone using only COBOL!

Artificial languages typically impose restrictions that are not to be found in natural languages. For example, in natural language there may be ambiguity. Individual words are often ambiguous, as in the case of the word *left* in the two sentences

> *He passed a train on his left.*
> *It left without delay.*

Sentences and phrases can be ambiguous too, as in the case of

Visiting aunts can be fun.

where there are two different interpretations depending on whether the aunts are visiting you or you are visiting them.

In artificial languages we can introduce rules to ensure that such ambiguity does not occur. For example, most programming languages have a defined set of reserved words which are words that the programmer cannot use for naming things. The need to handle ambiguity is one reason why processing a natural language is more complicated than processing an artificial one.

A second reason is that the structure of statements in artificial languages is usually kept very simple. In many programming languages, for example, statements are formed by applying an operator to one or more operands, or a function to a fixed number of arguments,

    a := b + 1;
    read (amends, quantity);

The same is true of more formal languages, such as propositional logic,

    not p
    q or (r and s)

The structures that appear in natural language are often far more complex. The opening sentence of George Eliot's *Middlemarch*, for example, is considerably more complex than anything you would expect to find in a Pascal or COBOL program:

> Who that cares much to know the history of man, and how the mysterious mixture behaves under the varying experiment of Time, has not dwelt, at least briefly, on the life of Saint Theresa, has not smiled with some gentleness at the thought of the little girl walking forth one morning hand in hand with her smaller brother to go and seek martyrdom in the country of the Moors?

Both types of language often allow one to describe the same object in more than one way. In Pascal, for example, the statement

    read (amends, quantity);

is equivalent to the code,

    quantity := amends ^;
    get (amends);

I want you to read the quantity from the file called amends.

Read 'amends' into 'quantity'.

The quantity is to be read from amends.

The reading of the quantity from amends is to take place.

Fig 1.1 A file read instruction described in various ways in English.

but the relationship between the two versions is simple and the equivalence is precise. Consider, by contrast, the various ways that one might describe that operation in English (see Fig 1.1).

In some respects the difference is a matter of degree. Natural languages are just very much more complex than artificial ones in the rules that they appear to use in their constructions. This greater complexity of structure makes the development of an adequate grammar and the building of an effective parser for natural language considerably harder than the processing of an artificial language in which the rules of construction can be kept relatively simple.

A third difference between artificial and natural language lies in the fact that because natural languages fulfill many functions it is very difficult to provide one way in which to represent the meaning of everything they can be used to express. By contrast, we usually design an artificial language with a specific objective in mind and this can help determine how we are to represent the meaning. Programming languages are designed so that programmers can write programs that will run on computers and this makes their meaning easier to define. We might say that the meaning of a piece of code in a programming language is the machine code that it produces to run on a computer. Purists may object that we have not specified which computer and that languages should be defined irrespective of any particular computer. This may be true but we do have at least the foundation upon which we can attempt to build a representation of the meaning of a program in a programming language.

Unfortunately, no such clear cut basis of meaning can be found for the variety of natural language utterances. Sentences in natural language can be used to describe situations, issue commands, ask questions, perform actions, deceive other people, express novel ideas, refer to themselves and do many other things. If it is difficult to find a satisfactory formulation for the meaning of a programming language, then how much harder it will be to do so for natural language.

If we distinguish between that part of a natural language processing system concerned with the structure of a sentence and that part concerned with the meaning of the sentence, then a further difference between artificial and natural languages emerges when we consider the relationship between these two parts. When we compile a program written in a language like Pascal, we first establish that the text is structurally valid. If we are successful we emerge with a single representation of the structure of each statement in the program, traditionally expressed in terms of tree-structure, sometimes known as a **parse tree**. Only when this is complete do we enter a second phase where we transform the structure into something meaningful, in this case the machine code that will run on some particular computer.

When using natural language we do not seem to make the same clear distinction between determining the structure and deriving the meaning. There are plenty of examples where our understanding of the meaning of the parts of a sentence is essential to our deciding how the sentence as a whole is structured. For example, the sentence

   John passed a train with a broken locomotive.

is structurally ambiguous. The phrase *with a broken locomotive* could be used to indicate that the train contained such a locomotive, or it could be used to indicate that John was driving a broken locomotive when he passed the train, or it could even be used to indicate that John was carrying a broken locomotive when he passed the train.

Unless there is a very special context, the latter two interpretations will be disregarded and the first adopted. This is because we know that you usually cannot drive broken locomotives and that locomotives are large and heavy and not the type of thing to tuck under one's arm. Hence we have to access the meaning of the constituent terms in order to determine the correct structure of the sentence. There is a debate about when we do this, but not about whether it need be done at all. This complication is almost always avoided in artificial languages, which makes the task of natural language processing that much more difficult.

To summarize, there are four major reasons why natural language is very much more difficult to process than an artificial language.

(1)   Natural language contains a great deal of ambiguity which is controlled in artificial languages.

(2)   Natural language generally has a much more complex structure than is to be found in artificial languages.

(3) There appears no simple universal way of representing the meaning of sentences in a natural language.

(4) Structure and meaning are necessarily interconnected in natural languages, whereas they are often separable in artificial languages.

1.2 Performance and competence

This is not to say that the techniques developed in dealing with artificial languages are irrelevant to processing natural language, but rather that such techniques are not enough. We need to pay attention to the specific features of natural language so that new techniques may be developed and applied appropriately. This means that we need to be clear as to our approach to language and what objectives we are setting ourselves in trying to process it.

During the 1950s Noam Chomsky redefined the discipline of linguistics by putting it on a more formal base. Central to this redefinition was his distinction between **linguistic performance** and **linguistic competence**. Chomsky observed that there is little consistency in the examples of language use we hear in our daily lives. Much speech contains interruptions, changes of direction, mannerisms, grammatical mistakes and a host of other features that make it a very poor basis for discovering underlying regularities. This type of linguistic behaviour, which he called linguistic performance, was seen by Chomsky as insufficiently stable to provide a sound basis for scientific study.

We rarely see examples of performance written down as text because most people make corrections and remove the irregularities of spoken language when they write, but you can see textual versions of linguistic performance in direct transcripts of events such as television or radio interviews. Fig 1.2 gives an example of linguistic performance as text.

Performance

That, err, man what I told you about - you remember, eh? - well he went and left, and straight away, like.

Fig 1.2 Textual example of linguistic performance

Even though adult users are inconsistent in their daily use of language, they are remarkably consistent at judging whether or not a particular string of words in the language is grammatical. That is to say, they can look at a string of words in, say, English and tell you whether it is a grammatical sentence or phrase. Most people, for example, can tell that the first sentence in Fig 1.3 is grammatical whereas the second is ungrammatical. Chomsky believes that this ability reflects our linguistic competence, our implicit knowledge of the grammar of our natural language. A scientific approach to language, according to Chomsky, involves an explanation of our linguistic competence, not merely our linguistic performance.

Competence

> Grammatical:
>> *He decided to leave immediately.*
>
> Ungrammatical:
>> ** He to decided leave immediately.*

Fig 1.3 Grammatical judgments are an example of linguistic competence

> Note: It is standard practice in linguistics to use the symbol * before a
>   text to indicate that it is ill-formed.

Chomsky further argued that the way that our linguistic competence is captured is by specifying a generative grammar. In general, **syntax** is a description of how words, and perhaps parts of words, combine together to form sentences. A **grammar** is traditionally a wider concept than syntax. A grammar can cover more than just the combination of words, it can also cover sounds (phonology) and meaning (semantics). A **generative grammar** typically relates to syntax and is a grammar capable of generating all the grammatical sentences in a language without generating anything that is ungrammatical. The term *generate* here is meant formally, in the sense that a generative grammar can specify how each valid sentence is constructed but it will not produce a specification for anything that is not a sentence. It is important to note that a generative grammar is not a grammar used specifically for generating sentences, in the sense of modelling their production. Chomsky's first major contribution to linguistics was to define its task to be to produce generative grammars for natural languages.

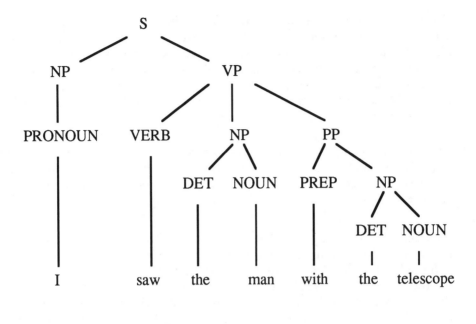

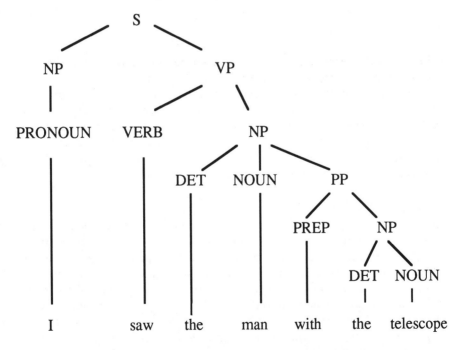

Fig 1.4   Two structural interpretations of the same sentence

If we had a generative grammar we should then be able to demonstrate the syntactic structure of any valid sentence or part of a sentence. Because natural language can be structurally ambiguous we may have more than one such structure for a particular sentence. If a sentence is unambiguous there should be just one structure, otherwise there should be a different structure for each possible syntactic interpretation of the sentence. Fig 1.4 shows two possible structural interpretations of the sentence *I saw the man with the telescope.*

Of course, building a generative grammar is not all there is to understanding natural language. It describes the structure of sentences, but not their meaning and whilst structure is clearly important in deriving meaning there is still another stage to go.

This second stage requires that we transform the output of a generative grammar into something that represents the meaning of the original sentence. Quite what the form of that representation should be and how we carry out the transformation is studied in the subject known as **semantics**. In the early days Chomsky tended to concentrate upon syntax and phonology rather than semantics, although semantic considerations were always relevant to his syntax. For other researchers, as we shall see, semantics has been a central issue.

While these theoretical developments were taking place during the 1950s and 1960s, computer scientists had been developing techniques to process the newly emerging programming languages. The programs that handled these artificial languages, called compilers, checked computer programs for grammaticality and made explicit the structure of the statements they contained. This development of techniques to handle artificial languages and the previously described work in theoretical linguistics combined to provide a strong paradigm for work in natural language understanding.

Historically, the objectives of natural language processing have been the production of a generative grammar which would take care of syntactic analysis and which would be accompanied by a semantic module that would take the derived structure and convert it into a representation of the meaning. The techniques used in this endeavour were those initially developed in computer science and subsequently suitably adapted. The four major differences between natural and artificial languages described above formed the research programme of the discipline. These involved dealing with ambiguity, structural complexity, semantic representation, and the interface between the syntactic and semantic components. This has remained the context in which most work in natural language processing has taken place.

1.3   Alternative views

Though the influence of generative grammar on natural language processing has been very strong, there have been some significant variations from it. Language can be seen as more than just a formal system described by a grammar. It is something that is used creatively, it is something that can be used (sometimes in surprising ways) to convey meaning, it is something that is processed by a real-time system and it is something we learn as well as use. All of these aspects of language (and we could have listed more) give rise to considerations that are beyond the formulation of a generative grammar.

Systemic grammarians, for example, have always maintained that it is impossible to analyse language separate from the context in which it is used. Language is not just a structure, but also a set of decisions that the speaker makes in phrasing a statement. For example, in referring to an event a speaker might formulate a question, a statement or a command, and if a question is chosen it may be a *yes/no* type question or a *wh*-type question. If it is of the latter type, it might be a *who, what, were, why* or *how* -type question. Systemic grammarians see the application of syntactic rules as revealing features of the structure which are useful to us when deciding how to complete the processing. The inclusion of features of structures has long been accepted as a necessary part of processing. For an introduction to systemic grammar see Morley (1985) and for a natural language processing system based upon systemic grammar see Winograd (1972).

If the objective of natural language processing is to arrive at a representation of the meaning of the sentence, then it may be wondered whether it is necessary to realize the syntactic structure at all. It may be possible to directly transform an input text into a representation of its meaning without going through the intermediate stage of a full and complete representation of the structure. In practice it may be necessary to pay some attention to syntactic structure, but this is not important. The crucial issue is whether syntactic processing is seen as an end in itself or is only used as and when it is required for semantic processing. A system of direct transformation into meaning representation would certainly not automatically produce the type of explicit structure shown in Fig 1.4. A prime example of this type of processing is to be found in Schank & Colby (1973).

Natural language is primarily processed by people, not computers, so in designing machines to understand natural language it is relevant to ask how human beings achieve their understanding. In order to improve the performance of parsers, some researchers have looked at human behaviour and have tried to build models that mimic human parsing, rather than models based upon the parsing of artificial languages. This has led them to build parsers which have the same limitations as human beings and that may even make the same mistakes. For example, we seem to be able to understand certain constructs up to a limit but beyond that limit they become overly complex. Most people can handle phrases like

> The dog the man owns
> The cat the dog chased

but have great difficulty if we start to extend the process,

> The cat the dog the man owned chased

If the objective is to understand human cognition then examples such as these are important cases to study. It may also be true that these limitations indicate how to design an efficient real time processor for natural language. An example of a parser that embodies psychological modelling is found in Marcus (1980).

Finally, there has been a recent revival of behaviourism with respect to natural language in the form of connectionism. Behaviourists seek to describe an ability such as linguistic competence in terms of a black box that is capable of displaying the behaviour associated with the ability. Hence they would not seek a generative grammar, but rather some mechanism that is capable of displaying competent linguistic behaviour. Connectionists have a particular view on the type of machine that should be used: it is basically a network of nodes that have weights associated with their connections. Hence, at least in the ideal form, a connectionist network can be given examples of grammatical and ungrammatical texts and, from these, can classify other examples correctly. Only the behaviour of the network is significant and the network itself may not be expressible in a symbolic form as, say, a generative grammar. One of the major advantages claimed for connectionist systems is that they are not limited to simple success or failure but can simulate various degrees of performance. For more about connectionist approaches to language see Zeidenberg (1990).

1.4 How the material is divided up

The topic of natural language processing by computer can be studied from the standpoint of linguistics (in which case it is often called **computational linguistics**) or from the standpoint of computing (in which case it is often called **natural language processing**). Whichever standpoint is adopted, the topics studied will be much the same. As suggested above, these may be categorized as four major problem areas.

(1) Building parsers that take a text and try to analyse it according to some grammar, bearing in mind the problems of ambiguity.

(2) Exploring different types of grammar and their suitability for representing the vagaries of natural language.

(3) Exploring ways of representing the meaning of a sentences so that, for example, an appropriate response may be made.

(4) Integrating the syntactic and semantic components in terms of an effective control structure.

Inevitably, the study of natural language processing relates to many other fields of study. Some of the major related areas are the theory of grammars, automata theory, data structures, logic and logic programming, psychology and the philosophy of language. Though our discussions may touch on some of these wider issues this book is primarily an introduction to the core areas of natural language processing.

We start Chapter 2 with a description of the ways in which speech may be analysed by computer. In order for speech to be input it must be represented as a digital signal and the first task is to break this signal up into representations of discrete sounds. From this we can build up a representation of what has been said, but it will be different from the textual version we might read from a page. It will be something like a phonetic representation but may also indicate other features, such as stress and pitch. From this, a textual version may be constructed.

The second half of Chapter 2 examines how words are composed. Though some words can be thought of as being atomic (e.g. *cat*), in that they have no parts and hence no complex structure, with others the internal structure of the word is very important. The word *unthinkingly*, for example, is made up from the root *think* and the additions *un-*, *-ing* and *-ly*, each of which tell us something about how the word should be used. This study of the way that words can be built up is called **morphology.**

We have already come across syntax and grammar, which is the topic covered in Chapter 3. In this chapter we will introduce the basic ideas of grammar, introduce a simple example, show some of the problems that make the formulation of a grammar for natural language so difficult, and discuss some of the approaches to grammar that have been adopted.

The discussion of grammar is kept separate from the discussion of **parsing,** which is the subject of Chapter 4. Parsing is the process of analysing a text with respect to some grammar in order to decide whether the text is grammatical and, if so, to make explicit its structure. Whereas a grammar is a purely formal system, a parser is a machine which operates for a period of time, performing some operations after others. This involves a new set of problems concerned with operations, data structures and efficiency.

Chapter 5 is concerned with semantics, or the representation of meaning. In simple terms it addresses the two questions, *What do we need to keep in a dictionary to correspond to the meaning of a word?* and, *How do the meanings of words contribute to the meanings of phrases and sentences?* That is to say, we are not concerned here with meaning in particular contexts so much as the literal or generally accepted meaning of a word or phrase.

Chapter 6 is about pragmatics and is concerned with other factors which may affect our processing of language, such as common sense or general knowledge. Topics covered here include the nature of dialogue, the context within which an utterance is situated and the role of common sense in communication.

Chapter 7 is concerned with the generation of text. If a system has something to say, perhaps in answer to a question, or to provide an explanation, then how does it put it into words that are both correct and sound natural in the context?

1.5. The sample text

As a book of this size cannot hope to cover all the issues in natural language processing, we have concentrated upon what we believe are the central issues for someone approaching the topic for the first time. As authors, this gives the book a coherence that we understand, but we recognize that for the reader this coherence may not be immediately obvious. In order to address this problem we have decided to base most of the examples in this book on the text of a single short simple story so that, for the novice reader, the book can be seen as a discussion of the issues involved in processing this particular text. Where we have not been able to use the sentences or phrases from the text directly to make all the points we would wish, we have used them as the basis of rephrasings.

Here is the text from which our examples are taken:

John woke to the sound of birds. It was the first day of his summer holidays and he was going to stay with his aunt who lived in Devon. Visiting aunts can be fun so he rang the station to discover the times of trains. A clerk told him that none of the trains were cancelled but one of them was already full. He decided to leave immediately.

He told his mother that he was going and ran to the bus stop. He saw a train at the station with a broken green locomotive. He boarded the Devon train with his luggage and it left without delay. John did not know that his aunt had already left her house. She was also going on holiday.

2

Speech, Phonology and Morphology

2.1 The analysis of speech

Speech analysis is an important aspect of today's emerging technology. Its purpose is mainly to perform two tasks: recognition (for input) and production (for output). Systems are being designed, for example, to perform interface roles to large on-line databases so that, hopefully, they will be more accurate than human information providers. Consider a train timetable as a database and a speech understanding system interfacing to this database. Users of the system would talk to the system down the telephone line and receive intelligent responses to questions, such as

I want to go to Paris from London on a weekday morning, what are my options?

The system must respond to this question in an intelligent and intelligible manner. It must thus both understand the question and produce an appropriate response. The meaning of the question must be extracted (see Chapter 5) from the user's question and when this has been done, the information it refers to must be represented in such a way that the user can understand what has been said. From the point of view of speech analysis the system must recognize what has been said as accurately as possible and then, when an appropriate response has been put together, respond as naturally as possible. It is beyond the scope of this text to deal comprehensively with this material, but most of the linguistic aspects of speech discussed here are necessary prerequisites to speech analysis.

In this chapter we shall look at how speech can be represented in a computer and how it can be classified at both the sub-word and word levels. This classification begins by defining a unit, the phoneme, which is defined by its ability to discriminate between words based on the sound made when the words are spoken. The phoneme itself may be analysed further into the different sounds that are made when producing it in different contexts. Rules can then be developed which will predict the correct sound to produce in any given situation. These topics are grouped under the title of phonology.

Words can be analysed in terms of their structure. Words such as *unknowingly* can be broken down into the units (or morphemes) *un, know, ing* and *ly*. As with the phoneme, there are rules for forming words from morphemes. This analysis is collectively known as morphology.

The chapter concludes with a discussion of the information loss in text processing due to our ability in our use of speech to convey much more than with the written word.

2.2 The representation of speech

Speech is produced by the passage of air from the lungs through the larynx into the vocal tract and out through the nose and mouth. This process generates sounds at many different frequencies which can be combined in a speech waveform (such as Fig 2.1). The waveform is continuous in both time and amplitude, and as such is known as an analogue signal. To store the information conveyed by such a waveform on a computer requires that this analogue signal be converted into digital form. This conversion tries to produce a discrete version of the continuous waveform.

The discretization of the waveform must take place in both time and amplitude. First, the waveform is sampled at discrete instants of time. This process produces analogue amplitudes at a fixed time interval. Then, the sampled amplitudes go through a process known as **quantization**, which produces the binary number representation of the original signal.

The basic idea behind **sampling** is to grab a value of the waveform at a predetermined rate, called the sampling rate. The value we are interested in is the amplitude (voltage level of the microphone) of the wave at that point (equivalent to its height above or below the axis). The rate is measured in terms of the frequency with which a grab is made, and is measured in Hertz (or cycles per second). The more grabs made the more information is retained and consequently the better the representation of the waveform. More grabs also means more data to deal with and so a compromise is often needed to find a sampling rate which will maintain accuracy but not be too expensive in terms of data processing.

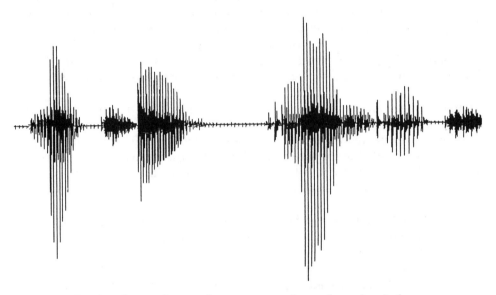

Fig 2.1 A speech waveform representing voltage levels from
a microphone measured 8000 times per second

A further complicating factor arises owing to the limitations of the sampling technique. Any signal is made up of a number of sine waves at different frequencies (Fourier's Theorem). Nyquist's theorem places restrictions on the range of those frequencies for a given sampling rate. The theorem is stated (somewhat informally) as:

A signal can only be faithfully represented if it does not contain frequencies that are greater than half the frequency at which the signal is sampled

Thus, if a sampler makes 10,000 grabs per second (10kHz) at the waveform then the sampled waveform should only contain frequencies in the range 0-5kHz. Frequencies above 5kHz would only serve to distort the sampled waveform. For this reason the analogue signal is normally pre-processed by a filter which removes frequencies above half the sampling rate.

To a certain extent this compromise has been settled by the various telecommunications companies around the world. Telephone networks only transmit frequencies in the range 300-3,400Hz. This range of frequencies is adequate for conversational purposes, although the quality of the speech is somewhat degraded by the transmission. Sounds which contain many high frequency components such as *s* suffer the most but it is still possible to both understand what someone is saying and recognise their voice. This range of frequencies means that for telephone quality speech a sampler running at 8kHz is adequate. The upper limit of human hearing is way above that offered by the telephone system, in fact it is about 20kHz. Consequently, for digitizing high fidelity music on a compact disc a sampling rate of 44.1kHz is used.

To make the amplitude discrete an analogue to digital (A/D) converter is used. This takes a voltage from a microphone and converts it into a number. The number represents the amplitude of the analogue signal. The accuracy of the conversion is related to the size of the digital representation used to store the voltage. If the size is one bit then the number of intervals in which this voltage can fall is two (0 or 1), with two bits the voltage can be classified as 0, 1, 2 or 3, and so on. Typically twelve bits are used giving 4096 values (or **quantization levels**) that can be used for the classification of the amplitude. Given that negative voltages are present then this gives a range of values between -2048 and +2047.

The result of this discretization process is thus a stream of numbers in some range determined by the quantization level produced at a rate determined by the sampling rate, and a knowledge that the frequencies contained in this stream lie between 0 and half the frequency of the sampler.

Computer storage needs for a speech signal can be calculated from the sampling rate and the quantization level by multiplying the two together. For example, with a sampling rate of 10kHz and an 8-bit A/D converter 8*10,000 bits (10,000 bytes) of information will be produced every second.

2.3 Phonetics

The spoken word has a great deal of similarity to its textual counterpart but can differ in significant ways. There are ways of using language which cannot be represented in a textual form. Playwrights, for example, have a considerable task in trying to get across their intentions using only the written word. Italics and punctuation can help but these are limited in their ability to indicate stress and intonation.   In this section we will examine this relationship and show how we can obtain a transcription of a spoken word into a textual form.

When dealing with speech on a computer one of the most significant things to remember is that it is extremely expensive to store and manipulate. A quality database of ten spoken words (the digits zero through nine taking 3 seconds) would require approximately 30,000 bytes of memory. The corresponding text (of 40 characters) requires only 320 bytes. The problem gets worse with speech because no one word is ever spoken twice in exactly the same way, not even by the same speaker. A speech database may also wish to incorporate several speakers who will have different vocal characteristics. There are significant differences between male and female speakers, for example.

One way to make savings in storage is to store a set of sound symbols which can be put together in some way to make words. We can make the observation that the *e*-sound occurs in seven of the ten digits, the *o*-sound in four, the *t*-sound in three etc. Thus, if we store the complete sound of each word we are using more storage space than is necessary. Text is cheap so we should make more use of it. Why not store each letter and put them together to form words?

This is a naive view to take, although for speech production sometimes this is the only option. You may have already foreseen some problems. However, there is something right about the strategy. If a set of sounds (not necessarily the letters) can be found then storage would not be as big a problem. The set of sounds would have to be big enough to generate all the words of the vocabulary we wish to cover, and also the sounds must be sufficiently different from each other to be able to discriminate between words.

What are the difficulties in using letters to represent sounds (and vice versa)? When using letters (i.e. the orthographic system) as the sound set an ambiguity problem occurs in both directions. A letter can represent more than one sound; consider the use of the letter *t* in the two instances in *station*. Conversely, a sound can represent more than one letter; a number of pairs of sounds can be seen to provide similar sound roles, for example the pair *c* and *k*, as in *clerk*. There are many other examples - you only have to recall the number of times that you have spelt a word incorrectly because you have used the sounds of it to make a judgement; some examples from this category are

    instance   - * *instence*
    separate - * *seperate*

where the first word in the pair is the correct spelling. What we want then is a set of symbols where one and only one symbol stands for each sound of the language, regardless of how the word is spelt.

Analysis of the way in which sounds are produced shows that there are something in the range of 10-20 articulators which can be varied to produce different sounds. These articulators include the lips, teeth, and tongue; each having several components and each having movements which vary continuously.

Combinatorially this means an infinity of possibilities, and yet as speaker and listener we somehow develop a system which isolates classes of sounds which we use for communication. It must be possible, therefore, to reduce the articulatory options to a finite number of classes of sounds. The study of systems which select and interrelate the sound patterns of a language is known as **phonology.**

The isolation of speech sounds is usually achieved by looking at either the way in which sounds are produced in the vocal tract (**articulatory phonetics**) or by looking at the properties of the waveforms emerging from the vocal tract (**acoustic phonetics**). The two are usually grouped together under the term **phonetics**. This excludes the study of the significant classes of sounds in a language and the rules that relate them, which is left to phonology.

The fundamental unit used in phonology for realizing a written representation of a set of sounds is the **phoneme**. The written representation of the set of sounds of a given language is called a phonemic transcription. Phonemes are abstract logical units whose function is to discriminate between words. Lists of phonemes can be built by choosing closely related words and finding the sounds that serve to discriminate them. For example, the *d, b, f, k, p* and *ch* in *din, bin, fin, kin, pin* and *chin* all belong to different phonemes.

The list formed in this way is somewhat bigger than the orthographic system although some letters keep their traditional values. Here we use a subset of the International Phonetic Alphabet (IPA). The IPA is capable of expressing any sound in any language. Our subset is based on the pronunciation of English used by speakers in the south of England, known as **received pronunciation** or RP for short.

Like the orthographic system, phonemes are usually classified as either consonants or vowels. From a sound production viewpoint this is perfectly reasonable. **Consonants** are articulated by placing obstructions (using the lips and tongue) in the path of air flowing through the vocal tract. For **vowels** very little obstruction occurs and the flow of air from the lungs to the mouth is relatively free flowing.   A summary of the phonemes used here is given in Fig 2.2.

Consonants = **b, d, f, h, k, l, m, n, p, r, s, t, v, w, z**

+ other symbols for consonant sounds

g	as in	*g-o*
tʃ	as in	*ch-ocolate*
ð	as in	*th-e*
j	as in	*y-es*
dʒ	as in	*j-ar*
ŋ	as in	*si-ng*
ʃ	as in	*sh-ow*
ʒ	as in	*deci-s-ion*
θ	as in	*th-eta*

Vowels:

short vowels		long vowels		diphthongs	
æ	as in *h-a-d*	ɑː	as in *h-ar-d*	eɪ	as in *pl-a y*
e	as in *h-ea-d*	iː	as in *h-ee-d*	aɪ	as in *h-i-d e*
ə	as in *a-loud*	ɔː	as in *s-aw*	ɔɪ	as in *t-oy*
ɪ	as in *h-i-d*	ɜː	as in *h-er*	eʊ	as in *h-oe-d*
ɒ	as in *h-o-d*	uː	as in *t-oo*	aʊ	as in *h-ow*
ʌ	as in *h-u-d*			ɪə	as in *h-e-re*
ʊ	as in *h-oo-d*			eə	as in *h-ai-r*
				aɪə	as in *h-ire-d*

Fig 2.2 Phonemes used in this chapter

When describing words in terms of their phonemic transcription the convention is to use solidi; thus *train* is written as

/treɪn/

The colon symbol (:) indicates a vowel of long duration. The vowel may be held for some time, a property often used in speech for emphasis, as in

This shirt was really /tʃiːp/.
That is /tuː/ *much.*

If the passage of air through the vocal tract is not obstructed in the production of vowel sounds then why is any sound produced at all? The answer is that the air flows through the vocal cords causing them to vibrate, and producing a buzzing noise. This buzzing noise is then shaped by articulators to produce a vowel. Sounds produced this way are called **voiced** and include both vowels and consonants. Hold your larynx and say some vowels: you should be able to feel the vibration. If the vocal cords are not used then the sound is said to be **unvoiced**. When you whisper, all sound is unvoiced.

Voicing is one aspect of the classification of phonemes into groups. This can be achieved by identifying sets of features that discriminate the groups or by configurations of the articulators. We do not have the scope in this text to cover these possibilities so only a sketch of this classification will be given. References at the end of the text indicate where to obtain more information.

Our treatment will begin with the consonants. When we speak, sound emerges from the mouth and the nose. If either or both of these are blocked the sound is stopped, at least momentarily. Two types of **stop** are distinguished depending on whether air escapes into the nasal cavity or not. If it does, then the stop is said to be a nasal stop or nasal, examples of which are

nasal stops:	/m/	as in	*mine*
	/n/	as in	*night*
	/ŋ/	as in	*ring*

When the nasal cavity is blocked the following oral stops, or simply stops, are distinguished.

oral stops:			
unvoiced	/p/	as in	*pin*
	/t/	as in	*tin*
	/k/	as in	*kin*
voiced	/b/	as in	*bin*
	/d/	as in	*din*
	/g/	as in	*grow*

When two articulators come close to each other a constriction is formed in the airstream. The resulting airflow is made turbulent and the sounds produced are hissing sounds. These hissing sounds are classified as fricatives, and like the oral stops are further subdivided by voicing.

fricatives:

unvoiced:	/s/	as in	*sin*
	/ʃ/	as in	*shin*
	/f/	as in	*fin*
	/θ/	as in	*thin*
voiced:	/z/	as in	*zebra*
	/ʒ/	as in	*decision*
	/v/	as in	*velum*
	/ð/	as in	*these*

When a stop is immediately followed by a fricative the sound produced is called an affricate.

affricates:

unvoiced:	/tʃ/	as in	*chin*
voiced:	/dʒ/	as in	*jam*

Liquids and glides are sounds similar in production to vowels. They are differentiated from vowels by shaping the vocal tract during the production of the sound; glides achieve this through vocal tract constriction, liquids through use of the tongue.

liquids:	/l/	as in	*liar*
	/r/	as in	*rascal*
glides:	/j/	as in	*yes*
	/w/	as in	*widow*

The phoneme /h/ as in *hinder* is the only **aspirate,** so called because breath is exhaled when the sound is made. Aspiration occurs elsewhere in speech production whenever breath is released. For example, when an oral stop is produced, air pressure is built up behind the lips and then released in a burst. Try putting your hand up to your mouth and saying the word *pencil.*

Vowels are classified in terms of tongue and lip position. For the tongue, consideration is given to its height (high, mid and low) and whether it is in the front, at the centre or at the back of the mouth when the sound is produced. For the lips two distinctions are made: vowels can be produced with lips rounded as in /tu:/ and unrounded as in /cæt/.

When the tongue position is moved from one position to another, within a single syllable, it is possible to produce a sort of concatenated vowel sound called a **diphthong**.   A summary of the short and long vowels is given in Fig 2.3.

iː	front high unrounded
ɜː	central mid-mid unrounded
ɔː	back mid rounded
ɑː	back low unrounded
uː	back high rounded
ə	central mid-mid unrounded
ɪ	front lower high unrounded
ʊ	back lower high rounded
æ	front mid-low unrounded
e	front mid-mid unrounded
ʌ	central mid-low unrounded
ɒ	back mid-low rounded

Fig 2.3 Long and short vowels

This classification can be plotted in two dimensions using the (front, central, back) classification as the x-axis and the (low, mid-low, high-low, mid, etc.) as the y-axis. The binary "roundedness" property is then indicated in this "space" by using a shading scheme of some kind. The resulting diagram is known as the vowel quadrilateral (see Fig 2.4).   Diphthongs, by definition, move around the quadrilateral changing their characteristics as they move.

Exercise 2.1

Try to produce a phonemic transcription of the sample text, here is a start:

/dʒɒn/ /waʊk/ /tə/ /ðə/ /saʊnd/ /aʊv/ /bɜːds/.

The **syllable** is the next highest meaningful unit used in language description. Syllables are the divisors of words, the **word** being the next highest meaningful unit after syllables. Syllables are made up of sequences of phonemes and, but for somewhat esoteric cases, always include a single vowel (or diphthong). The consonants of the syllable are said to cluster in sequences of one or more before and after the vowel, known as initial and final consonant clusters (respectively).

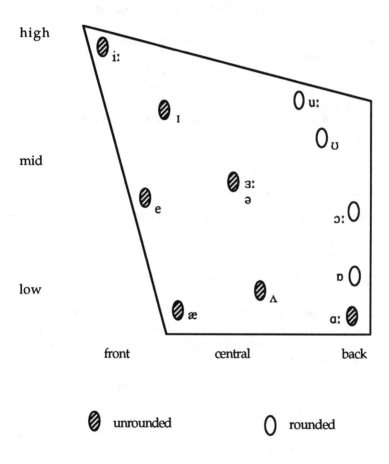

Fig 2.4   A vowel quadrilateral

2.4 Phonology

The phonemes we have described are not used in exactly the same way every time they are used in speech. Consider the word *tot* = /tɒt/. The phoneme /t/ is used, in entirely different ways; the initial /t/ is aspirated and the final /t/ is not (hold your hand to your mouth and say *tot*).

The context in which the phoneme is used is significant then in discriminating the sound made by the phoneme in a particular case. The actual sound produced when a phoneme is articulated is called a **phone**. For each phoneme there are many phones (which are also called **allophones**).

Allophones are not abstract logical units like phonemes - they are actual physical (acoustic) units, and as we have said there are many allophones to each phoneme.   We will use the convention of representing allophones in square brackets, [ ].   In order to predict the correct sound for a phoneme such as /t/ in context phonological rules are developed.   For /t/ we will propose six allophones (some of which may not be used by some speakers with RP):

[t1] =   at the start of a syllable as in *top*

[t2] =   at the end of a word as in *spot* (called a glottal stop)

[t3] =   preceding a nasal as in *bitten*

[t4] =   before an unstressed vowel and after a stressed vowel as in *gutter*

[t5] =   before a stop where the tongue touches the upper teeth (called a dental stop) as in *width*

[t6] =   when the sound is released as in *stop*

These can then be analysed in terms of distinguishing articulatory features, if they are voiced or unvoiced, aspirated or unaspirated and so on.   In order to distinguish the sounds phonetically, extra symbols are often added.   This process leads to rules such as,

[-voiced] [+stop] --> [+ aspirated] , when initial syllable

This rule applies to all the unvoiced stops /p, t, k/ and states that if these sounds occur at the start of a syllable then they will be aspirated.   That is the prediction that the phonological rule encodes.   Notice that it is a rule which applies to the allophones of /p, t, k/, not the phonemes.   In our example above it covers the [t1] allophone.   For [t2] the rule has an identical left hand side. There is no ambiguity, however, because the rules apply in different contexts.

[-voiced] [+stop] --> [- aspirated] , after /s/ at the start of a syllable

For vowels there are rules for predicting such things as their lengths and whether they are nasalized or not. The interested reader is referred to Ladefoged (1982) for more details.

2.5 The structure of words

In analysing a sentence of a natural language there are often a number of processing tasks which are involved. These are reflected, by and large, in the chapter structure of this text. Most natural language systems begin the process at the word level. The word is an extremely valuable unit to work with because it conveys information of use to most of the tasks. The word carries syntactic (Chapter 3), semantic (Chapter 5) and pragmatic (Chapter 6) information, all of which may be used in parsing (Chapter 4).

A word, however, is not atomic. Unless a word is entirely strange to a speaker, then he or she possesses the phonological knowledge to be able to pronounce it. The speaker may also know whether the word can be broken down into meaningful pieces. The word *unknowingly*, for example, can be further broken down while the word *train* cannot.

We also know that the plural form of this latter word is constructed from the word *train* and the plural ending *s*, and then there are variations on the verb *to train*, such as *training, trainer* and *trained* .

These parts of words, *train, s, ing, er, ed,* are known as **morphemes**. Some words have a very simple structure containing only one meaningful part; *train* is a good example of this. Any word which contains more than one morpheme is said to be complex. A complex word such as *training* has *train* as its **base** or **stem** or **root** morpheme and *ing* as an **attached** morpheme.

Some morphemes such as *s, ing, er* and *ed* are not words in their own right. For this reason these morphemes are said to be **bound**. A word such as *train* is not bound because it can be used as a word in its own right, and as such is termed a **free** morpheme.

Bound morphemes (called **affixes**) may be further categorized by whether they attach to another morpheme at the start or at the end. These are respectively known as **prefixes** and **suffixes**. All the examples of bound morphemes we have given so far have been suffixes. Examples of prefixes include *un* (as in *unhappy*), *re* (as in *rewrite*) and *extra* (as in *extramarital*).

Examples of words containing both prefixes and suffixes are *unfriendly*, *exchangeable* and *insignificantly*. Fig 2.5 lists the most widely used affixes in English.

prefixes: *a, ante, anti, arch, auto, be, bi, co, counter, de, dis, em, en, ex, extra, fore, hyper, in, inter, mal, mis, non, post, pre, pro, re, semi, sub, super, trans, ultra, un*

suffixes   *able, age, al, ance, ate, ation, cy, dom, ed, en, ence, er, ery, est, ful, hood, ible, ion, ing, ise, ish, ist, ity, ize, less, like, ly, ment, ness, ous, s, 's, s', ship, some, ster, teen, ty, ward, way, wise*

Fig 2.5 Mostly widely used affixes in English

Exercise 2.2

Work out the morphemes in the following examples:

bigger	*enormous*
gamekeeper	*illegitimate*
itemize	*lights*
she'll	*smallest*
synchronization	*trainee*

Exercise 2.3

You will find that morphology is rife with exceptions, and here is the first.   There are base morphemes which are not free morphemes (termed **base bound**); an example is the base morpheme *cran* in *cranberry*, an edible berry. (*Cran* can mean a measure for fresh herrings, but this is not the base used in this example.) Can you think of any other base bound morphemes?

If we look at the words of the phrase

he passed a broken green locomotive

we know that we can form further phrases such as

his locomotive

but not

* *his green*
* *his broken.*

Further distinctions can be made by noting that

* *he locomotive*

fails but

his carriage

succeeds.

We can thereby develop the notion of types of words, where an instance of a word in a valid sentence can be replaced by any other word of the same type resulting in a sentence that is still valid. We can see that *locomotive* and *carriage* are the same type of word, whereas *locomotive* and *broken* are not.

These different word types are known as **parts of speech**. They represent a classification of words based on their use within a particular language. A word may have more than one part of speech classification. In our sample text the words *sound, station, train,* and others all have more than one classification. The major parts of speech of English which we use here are:

nouns, pronouns, determiners, adjectives, prepositions, verbs, adverbs, conjunctions.

We will use them in this chapter to show certain morphological phenomena and also how a lexicon is constructed. If you are unsure of any of these classes an explanation of each one is provided at the beginning of Chapter 3.

Let us take a look at some rules for combining affixes to root morphemes. There are many rules and almost as many exceptions for English and so only some of these will be considered. The analysis is performed on an orthographic basis. Later in this section we show how the addition of phonemic information can assist morphological rules. We will concentrate on inflectional endings of words. Other types of affixes will be left as exercises.

Inflectional suffixes apply to nouns, adjectives and verbs and provide a good example of word formation rules. In each case the root morpheme is modified at the end. This may simply be the addition of a bound morpheme or may involve the deletion of the end of the root and the subsequent addition of a bound morpheme.

Consider the rules for plural formation of nouns. They are primarily concerned with the trailing letter(s) of the noun.   This will not be satisfactory for all cases as there are plural forms which are indicated by changes within the noun (irregular morphemes), as in *woman-women*, or where the plural form is the same as the singular form as in *sheep-sheep*.

Rule 1:   **If**   the word ends in *y*
                        and the penultimate letter is not a vowel
           then   the plural is formed by
                        deleting the *y*
                        and adding *ies*

(e.g. *lorry-lorries, story-stories*)

Rule 2:   **If**   the word ends with hissing sounds (called sibilants)
                        { e.g. *s* or *x* or *sh* or *z* or soft *ch* }
           then   the plural is formed by adding *es*

(e.g. *gas-gases, fox-foxes, fish-fishes, church-churches*)

Rule 3:   For all other nouns add an *s*

It is always helpful to write down the rules that cover the majority of cases first and then think of the exceptions.   These could include the irregular morphemes we mentioned earlier.

Exception 1:   **If**   the word ends in *o*
                then the plural is formed by
                either adding *s*
                or adding *es*

(e.g. *photo-photos, potato-potatoes*)

Exception 2:   **If**   the word ends in *i*
                then   the plural is formed by
                either adding *s*
                or adding *es*
(e.g. *taxi-taxis, chilli-chillies*)

Exception 3:   **If**   the word is child (irregular morpheme)
                then   the plural is formed by adding *ren*

Exercise 2.4

Can you think of any other exceptions where a suffix is involved?

What is peculiar about the example *fish*?

For **possessive nouns** the rule is straightforward,

Rule 1:   **If**   the noun does not end in *s*
          then   the possessive is formed by adding *apostrophe s* (*'s*)
          (e.g. *woman-woman's, women-women's*)

          else   the possesive is formed by adding an *apostrophe* (*'*)
          (e.g. *boys-boys', miss-miss'*)

For **adjectives** and **adverbs** there are two possible inflections, comparative and superlative.   Hence for the adjective *small* we have the comparative *smaller* and the superlative *smallest*.

Rule 1:   **If**   the word ends in *e*
          then   delete the *e*
                     and add *er* for comparative
                     or add *est* for superlative

          (e.g. *close-closer-closest*)

Rule 2:   **If**   the word ends in *y*
          then   delete the *y*
                     and add *ier* for comparative
                     or add *iest* for superlative

          (e.g. *lonely-lonelier-loneliest*)

Rule 3:   **If**   the word ending is a consonant
                     and is preceded by a vowel
          then   add a copy of the final consonant
                     and add *er* for comparative
                     or add *est* for superlative

          (e.g. *big-bigger-biggest*)

For **verbs** the inflectional suffixes are used to alter the form of the verb. The root verb form is known as the **infinitive**. A good general rule for saying if a verb form is an infinitive is to ask if the verb form can be preceded by *to*. Thus, *to have, to hold, to mother, to leave* all indicate correct infinitive forms. This can be coded in our lexicon; the entry for *have* may be of type **V-INF** (i.e. Verb-Infinitive).

The infinitive form provides no reference to a subject. The present tense form of the verb varies depending on whether the subject is singular or plural and whether the referent is the person speaking (first person), the person being spoken to (second person) or some other person or object (third person). For example:

	singular	plural
first person	*I move*	*We move*
second person	*You move*	*You move*
third person	*He moves*	*They move*
	She moves	
	It moves	

You can see that, for the majority of verbs, if we are dealing only with the present tense, the only inflectional suffix to the infinitive form involves the third person singular (e.g. *he moves, it rings, he carries, she boxes, he wrestles*).

The infinitive form also provides no reference to **tense** (i.e. time). This information is provided by changes to the infinitive form to produce the past tense (e.g. *I knew him*). Tense interacts with aspect. The continuous and perfect aspects, in contrast to the simple aspect, will be discussed in Chapter 3. Note for now that amongst the variety of verb forms we have:

simple past:
   (e.g. *I boarded, you carried, it passed*)

past progressive:
   (e.g. *I was boarding, you were carrying, he was passing*)

past perfect:
   (e.g. *I had boarded, you had carried, she had passed*)

Exercise 2.5

What happens to the part of speech classification and meaning of a word when an inflectional suffix is applied? A distinction can be made between suffixes which change the part of speech of the morpheme they attach to and those that do not, (**derivational** and **inflectional** suffixes respectively). From this definition and the table of suffixes write down lists of each type using the eight parts of speech above. What do you notice about the relationship of these two types when they are used together in complex words?

Exercise 2.6

Words can be constructed by joining two free morphemes together (a process called **compounding**); some examples are:

bedroom	*washing-up*	*backpack*
greatcoat	*bulldog*	*throughput*
stone-cold	*hit-man*	*freestyle*
oversee	*undercover*	*wash-up*

What part of speech is the compounded word in each of these cases? Can you develop a general rule for saying what part of speech should be given to new compounded words?

2.6 Building a lexicon

Having seen that some words are made up of base morphemes and affixes and that the latter can change the part of speech, we are faced with a choice. We can either store every known word in our lexicon with its part of speech (as in Fig 3.4) or we can store only base morphemes and write rules to process affixes and change the part of speech in the process. We shall consider each approach in turn.

The advantage of the former approach is that the word and its part of speech label can be identified without the need to examine the letters of the word, or perform any complex manipulation on the word. In Fig 3.4 the lexicon is presented in this way in a notation called a context free grammar.

In such a grammar the same style of rule that specifies the structure of words is also used to specify words, phrases and sentences.   This makes the overall processing of sentences simpler. A grammar for a language is specified in this notation as a series of lexical and syntax rules. Chapter 3 provides a more detailed description of context free grammar and lexical rules. We need the notation to explain our lexicon so we will restrict ourselves to necessary aspects.

A grammar is thought of here as a set of rules for showing the relationships between words. The term **context free** places a restriction on the formation of the rules. Essentially this restriction is that there can only be ONE symbol on the left hand side of a rule, though that symbol may appear as the left hand side of several rules. This symbol CANNOT be one of the words in the lexicon.

A context free grammar allows you to specify complicated **if-then** type rules. The complexity of the rules resides in the conditions of the **if** part. Consider, as a first example, the lexical rule

> DET ::= a | his | her | the

This rule reads as follows: a determiner (called **DET** for short) may be formed from *a* or *his* or *her* or *the*. The symbol | indicates alternatives. The symbol "::=" is read as *is defined as*. One view taken of these rules is that they represent re-write rules. In our example *a* or *his* can be re-written as **DET** by this rule. It is re-written in the sense that it may now be used as a **DET** in rules which contain **DET** on the right hand side, as in

> NOUN-PHRASE ::= DET   NOUN

This rule states that a noun phrase may be formed by a **DET** followed by a **NOUN**. If we work back to what a **DET** is this means that a **NOUN-PHRASE** can be formed by

> NOUN-PHRASE ::= a NOUN | his NOUN | her NOUN | the NOUN

If we were to now re-write the nouns (there are 24 even in our mini-lexicon) this rule would become very long. The context free notation therefore provides a powerful mechanism for describing the structure in a language.   Phrase and sentence level rules such as this are further described in Chapter 3 where the higher level structures of English grammar are discussed.

Returning to the **DET** rule above, in the **if-then** form this rule states

> **If**   the word is *a* or *his* or *her* or *the*
> **then**   label the word as a DET(erminer)

All the other entries in the lexicon are of the same type. Thus a lexicon written as a context free grammar is a set of rules which indicate the associations between words and their parts of speech (often called **syntactic categories**).

One thing to note about our lexicon is that it contains lexical ambiguity. Lexical ambiguity arises in a grammar such as this if a word appears on the right hand side of more than one rule. This means that a word does not have a single part of speech label, for example,

> V-INF ::= sound | station | ...
> V-EN ::= left | told | ...
> V-PAST ::= left | told | ...
> V-PRES ::= train | trains | ...
> NOUN ::= train | trains | sound | station | ...

This allows us to derive such rules as,

> **If**   the word is *station*
> **then**   label the word as a V-INF (Verb-Infinitive)
>   or a NOUN

If we do not want to store every word in our lexicon then we can store only base morphemes and write processes that will break a word down into its morphemes. A device that performs such an analysis is called a **morphological analyser**. A device that will create a morphologically complex word from its parts is called an **inflection generator**.

Let us consider the construction of an inflection generator. It is clear from the above rules that a program that returns the plural form of a noun given its root morpheme must be able to look at the last two letters of the root. This is most easily accomplished by treating the word as a list of letters, as in,

> [f,o,x]
> [p,h,o,t,o]

We will need to write utility routines to extract the last one or two letters from a list, to delete an item from the end of a list, and to concatenate two lists together. The Prolog code for these is given in Fig 2.6.

The rules (equivalent to Rule 1, Rule 2 and Rule 3 respectively) might be specified as in Fig 2.7.

```
last([L], L).
last([_ | L1], L) :- last (L1, L).


penultimate([L, _], L).
penultimate([_ | L1], L) :- penultimate(L1, L).


delete_end(X, [X], []).
delete_end(X, [Y | L1], [Y | L2]) :- delete_end(X, L1,L2).


concatenate([ ], L, L).
concatenate([X | L1], L2, [X | L3]) :- concatenate(L1, L2, L3).
```

Fig 2.6   Prolog general purpose routines

```
plural_noun(Root, Plural) :-
   last(Root, y), penultimate(Root, X),
   not(vowel(X)), delete_end(y, Root, NewRoot),
   concatenate(NewRoot, [i, e, s], Plural), !.


plural_noun(Root, Plural) :-
   sibilant(Root), concatenate(Root, [e, s], Plural), !.


plural_noun(Root, Plural) :-
   concatenate(Root, [s], Plural).
```

Fig 2.7   Prolog rules for creating plural forms

The exceptions occur as database entries which are searched first (i.e. placed above the rules in Fig 2.7). An example is,

```
plural_noun([p,o,t,a,t,o], [p,o,t,a,t,o,e,s]) :- !.
```

Exercise 2.7

Write a spelling checker program based on the morphological rules you have developed. Store only root morphemes and affixes. Write to a file all the words which fail the checking procedure and see if further rules are necessary. As an input file you could use the sample text.

Exercise 2.8

Write the full lexicon for the story. The first version should contain every word in the story and its syntactic category. The second version will contain only base morphemes and those rules necessary to correctly process every word. You can do this as a paper and pencil exercise or implement it in Prolog.

2.7 The use of morphology in text to speech production

One approach to the problem of generating speech from a textual description is to analyse the morphological structure of a word. Each morpheme and its associated pronunciation is entered into a dictionary. A word is analysed and broken up into morphemes, their pronunciations are retrieved from the dictionary and morphophonemic rules are used to piece the spoken word together. These rules indicate how morphemes influence each other when they are concatenated. They do this by altering the phonemic structure of the morphemes, placing the stress appropriately when the morphemes are adjoined, using rules developed by Chomsky and Halle (1968). An interesting aspect of these stress rules is that they apply mainly at the word level, with exceptions treated at the phrase level.

As an example consider the inflectional suffix *ed*. This has a different pronunciation depending on the sound which precedes it; *cracked, decided* and *bellowed* need morphophonemic rules to distinguish the /t/, /ɪd/, and /d/ endings. The dictionary items might be,

```
root_morpheme(crack, 'kræk').
root_morpheme(decide, 'dɪsaɪd').
root_morpheme(bellow, 'belaʊ').
```

The morphophonemic rules to cover these cases might be coded as in Fig 2.8.

% morpheme end is an unvoiced consonant

```
past_phonemic(Root, Past) :-
     last(Root, X),
     unvoiced_consonant(X),
     concatenate(Root, [t], Past).
past_phonemic(Root, Past) :-
     last(Root, d),
     concatenate(Root, [id], Past).
```

% morpheme end is voiced

```
past_phonemic(Root, Past) :-
     last(Root, X),
     voiced(X),
     concatenate(Root, [d], Past).
```

(n.b. "Root" is provided as a phonemic description):

Fig 2.8 Prolog code for morphophonemic rules

2.8 What we lose with text

Once we start to analyse speech we start to lose information. Attempts to make sound discrete inevitably lose some information but this loss is insignificant when compared to the loss of prosodic information in moving from speech to text.

Prosody is stress and rhythm applied to syllables and words to convey various types of information. It is concerned with features of speech above the level of the phoneme which span whole sentences. One such feature is the quality or fidelity of the sounds produced by a speaker. The quality is distinguished among speakers by the vocal apparatus used to produce the sounds. These anatomical differences (every piece of apparatus is unique) give some people "creaky" voices others "breathy" voices and so on. This is not as important to a natural language processor as other prosodic features.

The important prosodic features which are partially lost in text processing are stress and rhythm. In text we have the ability to specify these using commas for pauses, and exclamation marks, italics etc. for stress. These are useful but not comprehensive enough to specify the richness with which we use these features to convey meaning. Exclamation marks, for example, can only be applied at the end of a sentence, which is fine for one word sentences such as,

Help!

but not so good for,

He was only trying to be helpful when he said he would leave tomorrow!

Stress and rhythm are produced by variations in three vocal dimensions: pitch, time and amplitude. Amplitude (loudness) variation is not as influential as the others. Variation in pitch is known as intonation and this together with time variations produces what we think of as stress. Time variations include both the speed of delivery and the rhythm that is applied. The importance of these factors at the word level can be seen in the example of the word

appropriate

This is an adjective or a transitive verb depending on how the stress is placed on the last syllable (there is also a high degree of allophonic variation in this example).

At the phrase level a good example of this is (Lea, 1980)

She fed her dog biscuits.

The two meanings of this phrase rest in the stress placed on particular words or parts of words. This can have two meanings equivalent to,

She fed biscuits to her dog.

and,

She fed dog biscuits to her.

At the phrase level there is no way to distinguish these two meanings by text processing. The context in which this phrase was spoken provides the only clue.

It is possible to specify pitch in a limited way in text, for example with a question mark, as most questions involve rising pitch. In Australian and New Zealand English this is also true for statements. The unwary foreigner can be easily confused by this, thinking that all conversation is conducted in the style of yes-no questions and answers.

Perhaps the hardest prosodic features to recognize are those which convey emotional information such as sarcasm, rudeness, excitement, love, sympathy, etc. In reported speech these characteristics can be described very roughly using a qualifying word or phrase, for example,

"I have always cared for you Dorothy", he said lovingly.

These features are very important carriers of meaning and emphasise the subtlety with which language is often used.

In summary, prosodic features such as stress and rhythm are present in both speech and text. In text there are some indicators of this although they are not present at the word level. You will find examples of stress within words in a dictionary, where the symbol, ' , is commonly used to indicate that the syllable that follows it is stressed.

The stress and rhythm with which words are intended to be read are important pieces of information which are lost when the only communication is the written word . The absence of indicators for stress, in particular, leaves ambiguity in the text which can only be resolved by looking at the broader context in which the word or phrase falls.

For natural language processing systems which attach to a speech recognition front-end there is some hope of classifying parts of speech of ambiguous words if prosodic information is taken into account in the recognition process. In the future such systems may be able to detect the harder prosodic features which give natural languages their richness and subtlety.

Exercise 2.9

Where should the syllable stress marker be placed for the pronunciation of the following words:

below	*judgemental*
insecure	*dispute*
relativity	*haddock*
police	*solidarity*

Exercise 2.10

Name some words which can either be a noun or verb depending on how they are stressed.

2.9 Summary

We have shown in this chapter how speech can be stored on a computer, and how the various sounds of a language can be stored. English, for example, at the phonemic level requires the storage of approximately 24 consonant phonemes and 20 vowel phonemes. If allophones are used this number increases but not to the extent that it prohibits useful applications from being developed. Allophone-based speech synthesis, for example, is very common on many computer workstations.

Once we have a sub-word representation on the computer we can begin to use text processing techniques on the phonemes we have stored. We may combine them into syllables to form yet another representation, and then combine the syllables to form words. We have seen that words have structure, and by defining basic units (morphemes) it is possible to construct (or dissect) words into such units, leading to the coverage of an extremely large lexicon from only a small number of phonemes or allophones.

Text, unfortunately, does not convey as much information as the original speech, and this information loss has been discussed. For speech applications which hope to cover a large vocabulary and perform as naturally as possible there is a need to combine both text and speech processing techniques. In this chapter it has been our intention to indicate the importance of this.

An interesting feature of morphology is the way in which the syntactic categories of words can change when morphemes are added. These syntactic categories reflect a classification of words based on their use within a language. They are the starting point of text processing. The next chapter on syntax shows how similar classifications can be formed by combining words into phrases and, in turn, combining phrases into sentences.

3

Syntax

3.1 What types of word are there?

Syntax is the study of how words fit together to form structures up to the level of a sentence. In this chapter we shall look at some different kinds of word and the roles they play in sentence structures. We shall produce a context free grammar to handle the sentence structure of the sentences in our sample text and discuss some of the problems that arise in syntax. We shall also look at some alternative ways in which a grammar can be represented. We shall conclude by surveying a number of different theoretical approaches to syntax within linguistics.

We saw in the last chapter that words in a natural language such as English can be divided up into different kinds, such that all the words of a particular kind fulfill the same function within a sentence. This means that, given the sentence

John passed a green locomotive.

we know that words like *cabbage, armchair* and *house* are all the same kind of word as *locomotive* as they can be exchanged for it in that sentence and the result is still grammatical.

In traditional grammar these kinds of words are called **parts of speech**. Modern linguistics arrives at similar classifications for words but often refers to them as **syntactic categories**. We shall begin by explaining a little about the most common categories: noun, pronoun, determiner, adjective, preposition, verb, adverb, conjunction.

Nouns are traditionally understood as naming words. Examples of nouns in our story include *John, sound, birds, day, holidays, aunt* and *Devon*. *John* and *Devon* belong to a sub-category which we call **proper names**. In these cases the concept of naming is quite straightforward. The words are the names of particular things such as persons or places. Proper names behave a little differently from other nouns (known as **common nouns**) such as *sound* and *birds*, which can be thought of as naming whole classes of things to which the word can refer.

Modern linguistics does not define common noun or proper name in terms of a semantic (i.e. meaning-related) notion such as naming. Rather, the classification depends mainly on the idea of exchangeability. For example, I can say

> *The sound excited John.*

and I can replace *sound* by *birds, day, holidays* and *aunt*, but I cannot replace it by *Devon* or *John*. That is, I cannot say,

> * *The Devon excited John.*

Devon and *John* are therefore considered to belong to a separate class, principally because they are not preceded by *the* or *a*. Also they do not appear in the plural form.

Groups of words based on a noun are called **noun phrases**, for example:

> *it*
> *Mary*
> *his aunt*
> *the sound*
> *the loud sound*
> *a sound which was made by birds*
> *the very loud sound of music which was made by little yellow birds*
> ... *etc.*

Noun phrases can be used to describe things or classes of things. The principle of exchangeability still applies as each of the above phrases can complete the sentence that begins:

John was woken by .....

At first glance this looks like a very odd collection of structures but we can find some rules for defining them. Let us look at the various syntactic categories that can appear in or with noun phrases.

The first example, *it*, is a **pronoun**. Pronouns are a special case because they appear on their own in place of other noun phrases. Some common pronouns are:

I, me, you, he, him, she, her, it, we, us, them

Which one is used will depend on context, so, in the sentence

John gave a biscuit to his younger sister.

we can replace the noun phrases by pronouns and derive

He gave it to her.

There is another type of pronoun, known as a **relative pronoun**, which performs a joining function. They are words like

who, whom, which, that

and allow a noun phrase to be extended by adding a further phrase - typically a verb phrase (see below) or a truncated sentence. Two examples are

the man who liked John
the man whom John liked

We have already had occasion to mention words such as *the* and *a*. They appear at the beginning of a noun phrase and are called **determiners** because they tend to determine the way the phrase refers. They include the indefinite articles *a* and *an* and the definite article *the*. *His* and *her* (as in the phrase, *her house*) occur in similar positions and, though they are sometimes classified separately as possessive pronouns, we will count them as determiners because their behaviour is very similar.

Another group of words, sometimes called **quantifiers**, can also act as determiners. They are words like *all, some* and *none* as well as the numerals. Not only do they play a special role in semantics (see Chapter 5), but they also have the ability to introduce quantifying phrases, such as *all of the ...* or *none of the ...*

Adjectives (e.g. *green, dirty, broken*) modify a noun, thus providing a more specific description. A noun can be modified by more than one adjective. So we can have

    a locomotive
    a green locomotive
    a broken locomotive
    a broken green locomotive
    a broken dirty green locomotive

The final type of word that plays a major role in the construction of noun phrases is the **preposition**. Within noun phrases, prepositions behave in a similar manner to relative pronouns, in that they allow the modification of a noun phrase, but whereas relative pronouns allow modification by verb phrases or sentences, prepositions allow modification by other noun phrases. The meaning of a preposition often concerns possession, direction or location. Some common prepositions are:

    after, at, before, by, down, during, from, in, inside, of, on, outside,
    to, up, upon, with, without

Exercise 3.1

    Identify all the noun phrases in the short story. Identify all the parts of speech of the words they contain.

Let us now turn our attention to **verbs**, which are traditionally thought of as doing words, for example,

    delay, discover, have, know, leave, stay, stop

We have seen, in the previous chapter, that a verb can have many different forms. All the verbs in the list above are in the infinitive form.

Groups of verbs working together (known as **verbal groups**) are often regarded as the most significant part of the structure of a sentence. They have a very complex structure, not all of which we will be able to handle here. In English, verbal groups are used to handle variations of tense, mood and modality.

By the **tense** of a verb we mean where the event occurs in time: past, present or future. Connected with tense is **aspect**. There is the progressive aspect, e.g. *I am watching,* and the perfect aspect, e.g. *I have watched.* The combination of tense and aspect just by themselves generates a bewildering number of different verb forms.

I watch
I watched
I am watching
I was watching
I have watched
I have been watching
I will watch
I will have watched
I will be watching
I will have been watching

By the **mood** of a verb, we mean whether it is active or passive. Using the same verb, we get

| *I watch* | { active mood } |
| *I am watched* | { passive mood } |

as well as

| *I am being watched* | { passive mood } |
| *I will have been watched* | { passive mood } |

By the **modality** of a verbal group we mean indications of possibility or necessity or a degree of certainty. This is usually expressed by certain auxiliary verbs such as *can* and *may*. For example,

I can watch.
I may watch.

Sometimes a verb can be identical in written and spoken form to a noun. In the following sentences the bold words function as verbs but the same words are used as nouns in our sample text.

*Does this **sound** nice?*
*They wanted to **station** me in Devon.*
***Stop** that!*
*They are going to **train** me.*
*I would like to **holiday** in Devon.*

Here are a couple of sentences in which the bold nouns correspond to verbs in the text.

> *Have a nice stay!*
> *His politics were on the left!*

Adverbs usually qualify verbs in much the same way that adjectives qualify nouns. In

> *He decided to leave immediately.*

the adverb *immediately* qualifies the verb *leave*.

Finally, **conjunctions** are connecting words, e.g. *and, but* and *so*. They can be used to join two simple sentences into a compound sentence, as in

> *He boarded the Devon train and it left without delay.*

The conjunction *and* can be used to join other types of phrase, such as noun phrases and verbal groups. For example,

*He washed **his shirt and his socks**.*	{compound noun phrase}
*He washed **and ironed** his shirt.*	{compound verb group}

Exercise 3.2

Identify the part(s) of speech for every word in the sample story.

3.2 Describing the structure of sentences

Implicit in these brief descriptions of word classes is the notion that the words of a sentence fit together in certain patterns. A sentence can be regarded as being composed of a relatively small number of building blocks (say, two or three) which are called its **immediate constituents**. These constituents themselves have their own immediate constituents and so on until we get down to the level of the word.

A **phrase** is a constituent smaller than a simple sentence, so we might say that the sentence

> *He packed his bags.*

consists of two phrases, *He* and *packed his bags*, and that the latter phrase consists in turn of two phrases, *packed* and *his bags*.

Sometimes a constituent of a complex sentence has a sentence-like structure itself. In this case it is commonly called a **clause**. An example is the clause *none of the trains were cancelled* in

   A clerk told him that none of the trains were cancelled.

Without using labels, one could express the constituent structure of a sentence in a tree diagram such as Fig 3.1.

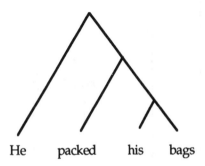

He   packed   his   bags

Fig 3.1   The constituent structure of a sentence

It is far better to employ labels on such trees to reflect the phrase or word type that appears there. Using some phrase names that we will explain later, we derive the diagram in Fig 3.2.

All points on the tree which contain a label or a word are called **nodes** (i.e. S, NP, VP, PRONOUN, VERB, POST-VERB, V-PAST, DET, NOUN, *He*, *packed*, *his*, *bags*). The single node at the top is called the **root node** and the nodes at the bottom containing the words (and which have no further constituents) are called **leaf nodes** or **terminal nodes**. A node **dominates** another node if there is a direct path downwards through the tree from the first node to the second. Thus in Fig 3.2 the rightmost **NP** dominates both *his* and *bags*. It also immediately dominates **DET** and **NOUN**. Where two nodes are immediately dominated by the same node they are **sister nodes**, so **DET** and **NOUN** are sister nodes. Note that the words themselves only appear on terminal nodes and the non-terminal nodes contain labels of abstract syntactic categories. Words appear in diagrams as lower case and if they are used in the text they will appear in italics. Labels are capitalized in diagrams and are printed in bold in the text to help distinguish them.

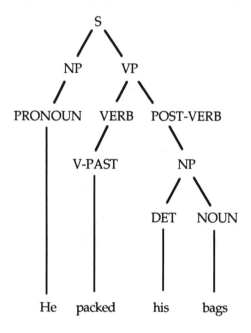

Fig 3.2   A labelled constituent structure diagram

3.3 A context free grammar

We became familiar with the idea of a context free grammar in Chapter 2 and now it is time to build one. A grammar that is powerful enough to be able to analyse all English sentences is an impossibly large and complex task, so we will not try to do that here. Rather, we will try to develop a grammar that will meet the following three criteria.

(1) It will be able to analyse all of the sentences in our sample text (and show different analyses where a sentence is ambiguous).

(2) It will not generate too many sentences that are ungrammatical in English.

(3) It will use phrases and rules that are generally applicable, even if in some cases they involve a gross simplification of the way English works.

Fig 3.3 contains the context free grammar that will serve as an extended example. (The numbering of the rules, 1 - 24, is to make it possible to refer to them simply and is not an èssential part of the grammar.)

1	S ::=	NP VP	
2		NVP VP	
3		S CONJ S
4	NP ::=	PRONOUN	
5		PROPER	
6		[DET] ADJ* CLASF* NOUN PP* [REL-CL]	
7		QU-PH NP	
8		NP and NP
9	QU-PH ::=	QUANT of
10	CLASF ::=	NOUN	
11		PROPER
12	PP ::=	PREP NP
13	REL-CL ::=	REL-PRON VP
14	NVP ::=	V-ING POST-VERB
15	VP ::=	[MODAL-PH] [HAVE] BE [ADVB] ADJ	
16		[MODAL-PH] [HAVE] [BE] [ADVB] VERB POST-VERB	
17		VP and VP
18	MODAL-PH ::=	MODAL	
19		MODAL not
20	POST-VERB ::=	[ADVB] [NP] [V-MOD]
21	V-MOD ::=	PP* [TO-PHRASE]	
22		PP* that S
23	TO-PHRASE ::=	to V-INF POST-VERB
24	VERB ::=	V-INF	V-ING	V-PAST	V-PRES	V-EN

Fig 3.3 A context free grammar for the sample story

There are four symbols used in the definition of this grammar that need explaining.

::=   This can be read as *is defined as* or *is re-written as* (see below).

| This can be read as *or*. Rules 1, 2 and 3 could have been written separately as:

   1 S ::= NP VP
   2 S ::= NVP VP
   3 S ::= S CONJ S

But in Fig 3.3 all the rules with S on the left hand side are compressed into one rule with | separating the options.

[ ]   Square brackets around an item mean that its presence is optional. Hence a rule

   NP ::=   [DET] NOUN

would be the same as

   NP ::=   DET NOUN |
            NOUN

*   An asterisk after an item means zero or more occurrences of the item. Hence a rule

   NP ::=   NOUN PP*

is a way of saying one NOUN followed by any number of PPs.

A formal account of context free grammars is available in Gazdar & Mellish (1989) and in most introductory computer science texts. We should observe that the grammar is composed of unstructured symbols. Thus NP, while suggesting the words *noun phrase*, is formally speaking a simple symbol, which could be replaced by X, for example. In each of the rules there is one symbol to the left of the ::=, indicating that the re-writing does not depend on surrounding context, hence the phrase **context free**. As noted above, terminal symbols cannot appear to the left of ::=.

A **lexicon** is a list of words and their syntactic classes. The lexicon for the grammar is given in Fig 3.4.

DET ::=	a I his I her I the
QUANT ::=	one I some I all I none
ADJ ::=	V-EN I V-ING I
	first I full I fun I green
NOUN ::=	aunt I aunts I birds I bus I can I clerk I day I delay I
	holiday I holidays I house I left I locomotive I luggage I
	mother I others I sound I station I stop I summer I times I
	train I trains
PROPER ::=	Devon I John
PRONOUN ::=	he I him I it I she I them
PREP ::=	at I in I of I on I to I with I without
REL-PRON ::=	that I who
CONJ ::=	and I so
MODAL ::=	can I did I may
HAVE ::=	had I has I have
BE ::=	am I be I been I is I was I were
V-INF ::=	be I delay I discover I go I have I holiday I house I know I
	leave I mother I sound I station I stay I stop I train
V-PRES ::=	am I delay I discover I go I goes I has I have I holiday I
	holidays I house I is I know I leave I lives I mother I sound
	I station I stay I stop I train I trains
V-PAST ::=	boarded I cancelled I decided I had I left I lived I passed I
	ran I rang I told I was I went I were I woke
V-EN ::=	been I boarded I broken I cancelled I decided I gone I had I
	left I lived I passed I told
V-ING ::=	being I going I having I visiting
ADVB ::=	already I also I immediately

Fig 3.4 The lexicon for the sample story

As we will see in Chapter 4, this grammar can generate the set of sentences in the sample text together with tree structures, as in Fig 3.2. This sort of tree is sometimes known as a **phrase marker**. The way the grammar generates the sentences and trees is to start with the specified initial symbol, **S**, find a rule which contains it on the left hand side, say rule 1.

1   S ::=   NP VP

This says that the **S** can be rewritten as **NP VP**. This rule follows the traditional division of a sentence into subject and predicate. It is represented by the top layer of the tree, as in Fig 3.5.

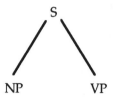

Fig 3.5 Tree representation of: S ::= NP VP

Next the grammar finds a rule with **NP** on the left hand side, re-writes that and repeats the operation for **VP**. The process continues until we are left with only terminal symbols, the words of a sentence. Chapter 4 will explain how this process is used to analyse a given sentence using a parser.

Let us consider how noun phrases are made up, to make it clear why the rules for NP in the grammar (rules 4 to 8) are the way they are. In our grammar, proper names (**PROPER**) and pronouns (**PRONOUN**) stand by themselves as noun phrases (in Rules 4 and 5 respectively).

Exercise 3.3

Rules 4 and 5 allow the following to be noun phrases:

Devon	*John*	*h e*	*him*
it	*she*	*them*	

In English, is it really correct that any of these words can appear wherever there is an **NP** symbol in the grammar? If not, what limitations are there on their use?

Rule 6 expresses the fact that many noun phrases are headed by a noun with various optional elements that can come before or after it. If you look carefully, you will find that **NOUN** is the only compulsory item on the right hand side of that rule. For example, whilst the single word *locomotives* can be a complete noun phrase (as in *locomotives are noisy and smelly*), to handle a noun phrase such as *the old locomotives* we need an optional determiner (**DET**) and an optional adjective (**ADJ**) to precede the **NOUN**. But there can be more than one adjective, as in *the broken old locomotives*. Expressed as a rule in a context free grammar these observations lead us to

NP ::= [DET] ADJ* NOUN

Looking at our lexicon, we can see that this rule will allow us to generate, among many other phrases,

birds
a bus
his first holiday
the first green train

But it will definitely not allow us to generate as noun phrases such strings of words as

* *the*
* *bus a*
* *the his holiday*
* *the train green first*

As yet our rule does not accommodate

his summer holidays
the Devon train

even though they are grammatical English (and contained in our story). Nouns and proper names (here *summer* and *Devon*) are also able to qualify the head noun and we call these classifiers (**CLASF**). As there can be more than one such classifier (as in *his Devon summer holidays*) we can use the asterisk to give us **CLASF ***.

The noun phrase *the first day of his summer holidays* includes the prepositional phrase (**PP**) *of his summer holidays*. Prepositional phrases are simply composed of a preposition and a noun phrase, which in the form of a rule is

12   PP ::= PREP NP

(This gives us one example of how a noun phrase can be contained within a larger noun phrase.)

Our rule for noun phrases is now

NP ::= [DET] ADJ* CLASF* HEAD PP*

This will generate more complex noun phrases, such as

the summer holidays in Devon
the first sounds of the summer
the luggage in the green bus at the station

Here is a final aspect of Rule 6. Any of the noun phrases we have generated so far can have a relative clause (**REL-CL**) added to the end. A relative clause begins with a relative pronoun (see above) which is followed by a verb phrase (see below). The rule that defines them is

13   REL-CL ::= REL-PRON VP

The following are relative clauses by this definition

who lives in Devon
who trains birds in his holidays
that is at the station

Rule 7 shows how a noun phrase, such as *the summer holidays,* can be preceded by a quantifying phrase (**QU-PH**) such as *all of, none of* or *some of,* making *all of the summer holidays, none of the summer holidays* and *some of the summer holidays.*

Rule 8 allows us to make compound noun phrases such as

the first bus and the green locomotive

The final description we give of noun phrases, through Rules 4-8, is quite complex but should still not be regarded as a definitive specification of noun phrases in English. A perfect grammar would generate all AND ONLY the noun phrases of English. Our grammar, unsurprisingly, fails to generate all the noun phrases of English, but also fails to generate only grammatical English noun phrases.

Exercise 3.4

Find a string of words that is specified as an NP by our grammar but would not qualify as a grammatical noun phrase in English, according to your own judgement. Suggest a way of amending the definition of **NP** to accommodate your example.

At the heart of every verb phrase is the verb group. Verbs are said to come in various **tenses**, primarily: past (**V-ED**), present (**V-PRES**), and future (using **V-INF**) as in,

past:	*He rang ...*
present:	*He rings ...*
future:	*He will ring ...*

These are said to reflect the time of the situation described in relation to the time of its utterance. Note that the future tense is a little different from the others in English as it involves an auxiliary verb, in this case *will*.

Tense interacts with **aspect**. The **progressive** aspect is constructed using a form of the verb *to be* (**BE**) and the present participle (**V-ING**) form of the verb that follows. This gives us:

past + progressive:	*He was ringing ...*
present + progressive:	*He is ringing ...*
future + progressive:	*He will be ringing ...*

The **perfect** aspect is constructed from a form of *to have* (**HAVE**) and the past participle (**V-EN**) form of the verb that follows. Thus the three tenses for *ring* in the perfect aspect are:

past + perfect:	*He had rung ...*
present + perfect:	*He has rung ...*
future + perfect:	*He will have rung ...*

Moreover, the perfect and and progressive aspects can work together to produce the forms:

past + perfect + progressive:	*He had been ringing ...*
present + perfect + progressive:	*He has been ringing ...*
future + perfect + progressive:	*He will have been ringing ...*

In these examples note that the presence of a form of *have*, indicating perfect aspect, requires that *be*, which follows it in these cases, changes to the past participle *(been)*.

Passives are created with a form of the verb *to be* (**BE**) and the past participle (**V-EN**). In the three tenses this gives us:

past + passive:	*The station was rung ...*
present + passive:	*The station is rung ...*
future + passive:	*The station will be rung ...*

Once again, this can interact with different aspects to give us, for example:

past + perfect + passive:	*The station had been rung ...*
present + progressive + passive:	*The station is being rung ...*

Once again, the form of *be* in the formation of the passive is affected by the presence of the aspectual *have* or *be* preceding it.

We have already mentioned **modal** auxiliaries such as *can, may, might* and *must*. They also have to fit into the verb group, giving us such combinations as

> *He must have rung* ...
> *The station may be rung* ...

See how the modal auxiliary is always followed by a verb in the infinitive form (**V-INF**).

To produce a grammar simply for verb groups is quite a task in itself. Our grammar does not attempt that in a rigorous way. It allows all the verb groups in our text to be produced, but it allows many unacceptable combinations as well.

Exercise 3.5

Find a verb group that is specified by our grammar as a **VP** (without a **POST-VERB**) but is not a grammatical verb group in English.

Finally we will look briefly at what might follow the verb group in the verb phrase. Suppose the grammar has taken Rule 1 and then Rule 16:

16 VP ::= [MODAL-PH] [HAVE] [BE] [ADVB] VERB POST-VERB

If it doesn't take any of the bracketed options and just produces **VERB POST-VERB**, then the phrase marker is as in Fig 3.6.

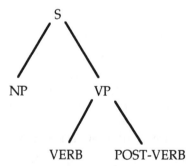

Fig 3.6 Phrase marker after Rules 1 & 14

The rule for **POST-VERB**, Rule 20, gives us various options. Suppose the grammar selects just **NP** from those options. That **NP** within a **VP** is called the **direct object**. In English, not all verbs can take a direct object. One that can is called a **transitive verb**. The verb *to tell* is a transitive verb as in, *He told his mother*. A verb that cannot take a direct object is called an **intransitive verb**, for example the verb *to decide*. Fig 3.7 compares the expansion of **POST-VERB** for parts of the sixth and fifth sentences of our text.

Exercise 3.6

Our grammar does not involve a distinction between transitive and intransitive verbs. Find some sentences that are generated by the grammar but are unacceptable because they include a direct object for a verb that is really intransitive.

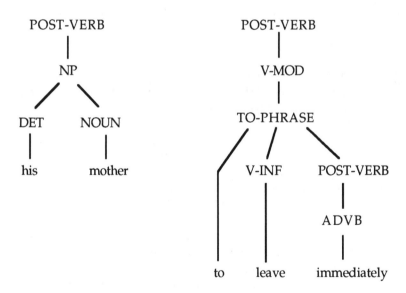

Fig 3.7 Comparison of POST-VERB structures

As we have been seeing, linguists aim to construct a generative grammar that generates precisely the sentences of some dialect of a natural language. The structural descriptions of the sentences should be appropriate and at least bring out the recognized structural ambiguities in sentences of the language.

But maybe there is a further and deeper goal the linguist should aim for in writing a grammar of a language. Maybe all human natural languages share some significant universal properties that reflect an innate language faculty in humans. If so, it may be appropriate to write a grammar in a form that reflects that language faculty. Chomsky has been urging such a view on the linguistics community since the 1960s.

3.4 Why is syntax a problem?

As described in Chapter 1 natural languages are significantly different from artificial languages. Part of the difference lies in the way syntactic forms encode meaning. For example, we all know that one word can have several meanings (e.g. *train* could mean *a series of carriages pulled by a locomotive* or *the trailing part of a wedding gown*). This is known as **lexical ambiguity** as it is the lexical unit (i.e. the word) that is ambiguous. In both of these meanings *train* is a noun.

This leads us to a peculiarity of natural languages with greater relevance for syntax. Sometimes a word (that is, the same spoken and written form) appears in two parts of speech. Several words in our story can function as both a noun and a verb (e.g. *sound, stop, holiday, stay*) though in these cases the two meanings are related. Sometimes the two functions have unrelated meanings. *Train* can also be a verb meaning *to instruct*, which is largely unrelated in meaning to *train* as a noun. As the form of the word does not uniquely determine its syntactic category in natural languages it is left to the linguistic context to do so. These cases can be described as lexical ambiguity, too.

Another form of ambiguity, which depends critically on syntactic structure, is called **local ambiguity**. Here, a string taken out of the context of a sentence would have one form and meaning while in the context of the whole sentence it would have a quite different structure and significance. In the sentence

Someone who likes summer arrives quickly.

the string, *summer arrives quickly* qualifies as a simple sentence if taken by itself but does not have that structure within the context of the sentence. In fact it is not even a constituent (i.e. it is not dominated by a single node in the tree). Local ambiguity is a form of structural ambiguity in that it depends on there being different analyses of the syntactic structure of a string of words.

One word belonging to two syntactic categories may help create this situation. In the sentence

   Is John left of centre?

the words *John left*, taken by themselves, could be a simple sentence. However, in the broader context of the whole sentence it is clear that *left of centre* must be taken as a noun phrase and *John left* is not a constituent of the sentence.

Sometimes the structural ambiguity is not resolved at the level of the whole sentence as in the example from the text,

   Visiting aunts can be fun.

This is called **global ambiguity**. This type of ambiguity cannot be resolved by the grammar but should be able to be demonstrated, by presenting two different structures corresponding to the two possible interpretations of the sentence, as in Fig 3.8.

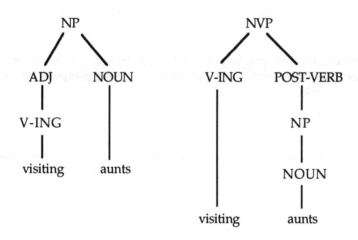

Fig 3.8 Two interpretations of *visiting aunts*

None of these ambiguities are typically present in artificial languages. When we come to parsing in the next chapter we will see how much difficulty ambiguity leads to.

Another general problem in natural language syntax is **ellipsis**, where a longer structure is abbreviated. One case of that has been called **gapping**, where a repeated word or phrase is eliminated. For example,

> *Mary tidied up the kitchen and John _ the living room.*

The indicated gap shows where the repeated phrase, *tidied up* was eliminated. Another example would be

> *She delivered two boxes of catfood and one _ of apples.*

Such elliptical forms represent whole new patterns. One way to try to deal with them is to handle the unabbreviated forms and then provide rules of abbreviation.

We have already mentioned how a noun phrase can contain another noun phrase. We can speak of the contained phrase as being **embedded** in the containing phrase. The same terminology applies to other cases of containment, where the contained phrase is either of the same kind as the phrase in which it is embedded or of the same kind as a node which dominates the phrase in which it is embedded. We can speak of a sentence being embedded in a noun phrase, in the form say of a relative clause (e.g. *his aunt who lived in Devon*) but we cannot speak of a noun phrase being embedded in a sentence.

A context free grammar can handle one kind of embedding by having recursive rules where the same symbol appears as part of the right hand side as appears on the left hand side.

> 3   S ::= S CONJ S

This can license indefinitely large sentences, for there is no limit to the number of times the rule can be reused, building up larger and larger sentences like this

> *John woke.*
> *John woke and his aunt sang.*
> *John woke and his aunt sang and the porter whistled.*
> ... and so on.

Note that there has to be a non-recursive way of rewriting S as well, such as,

> 1   S ::= NP VP

or we would never get away from the one rule and get on to the rest of the grammar (see Section 4.2). There may be a group of rules that act together to produce recursion such as the recursive pair of rules

```
NP ::= DET NOUN PP*
PP ::= PREP NP
```

This can generate, for example,

his luggage at the bus stop by the station

and

the picture on a wall in a picture on a wall in a picture ....

It appears that people can only understand (and produce) phrases with a limited number of embeddings, but it is interesting that different forms of embedding appear to be quite different from the point of view of comprehensibility, as was pointed out in Chomsky (1965). There are several layers of embedding in the noun phrase

John's aunt's friend's ticket

as can be seen in the unlabelled tree diagram in Fig 3.9.

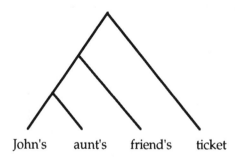

John's   aunt's   friend's   ticket

Fig. 3.9 Structure of embedded phrases

Such a structure, known as a **left branching** structure from the look of the tree, tends to be more readily comprehended than a **nesting** structure where the contained part comes in the middle of the larger structure. Consider the noun phrase

the porter the children John recognized pointed out

i.e.

the porter (whom (the children (whom John recognized)) pointed out)

This is much harder to comprehend. Part of the difficulty relates to the way the phrase *the children John recognized* is embedded in the middle of the larger phrase. That the *whom*-structure is repeated makes matters worse.

According to Chomsky the differences in acceptability of different kinds of embedding is part of the study of performance and does not affect the grammaticality of the sentences. Chomsky's notion of performance also concerns a range of other phenomena, as illustrated in Fig 1.2. There are a whole host of stumbles, mix ups and half finished sentences which appear in ordinary speech. Making a distinction between competence and performance allows one to ignore such things in the construction of a grammar. But when it comes to processing real natural language input, particularly in spoken form, they have to be dealt with.

3.5 Representing a grammar

Our example grammar was represented as a context free grammar. This is a mathematically well understood system that is computationally tractable.

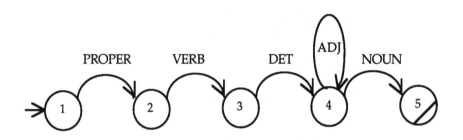

Fig 3.10   Finite State Transition Network (FSTN)

However it may be appropriate to introduce a style of grammar which is computationally simpler and see what developments need to be made to accommodate the needs of natural language processing. Consider a simple grammar expressed as a finite state network (see Fig 3.10).

This grammar, as it is appropriate to call it here, consists of a finite number of states, including a **start state** and an **final state**, indicated here by,

start state   final state

and various arcs between states. An arc represents a transition between states. That is, you move between states across those arcs in the direction of the arrow. In our example each arc has a label attached, the label being a class of words of the language. The idea is that at any state in the network there is a specified range of next moves which represent the words that could come next in the sentence.

Suppose, for simplicity, the word classes are

> PROPER: *John, Mary*
> VERB: *boarded, cancelled, saw*
> DET: *the, that*
> ADJ: *old, grey*
> NOUN: *bus, taxi, train*

Then the sentences specified by the grammar include

> *John boarded the train*
> *John boarded the old train*
> *John boarded the old old train*
> *Mary saw that grey old bus*

Exercise 3.7

Produce several more sentences that are specified by the network and some sentences not produced by the network that you judge to be grammatical in English.

Clearly it would be extremely messy to construct a finite state transition network in that style to cope with even just the sentences in our story. One thing that would be clearly desirable would be for the labels in the network to stand for not just classes of words but also kinds of phrases. Noun phrases, for example, can occur in various parts of a sentence; amongst other positions, they can occur as subject and direct object, so one could have a simple sentence of the form,

NP VERB NP

Rather than duplicate all the possibilities with respect to noun phrases we could have a separate network for noun phrases (labelled NP) and just have NP appear twice in the original network, as in Fig 3.11. If we have a set of networks in this way we have a structure much more like the context free grammar we have been using all along.

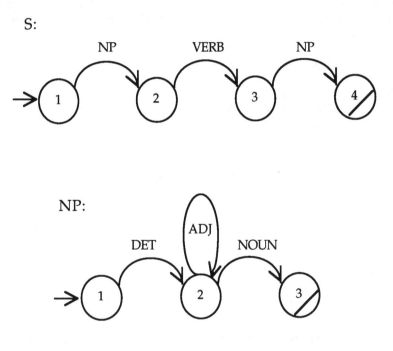

Fig 3.11 A set of finite state transition networks

We saw before how noun phrases can contain noun phrases. Once we have a set of networks with labels we can easily construct a network containing an arc labelled with the same name as that of the network in which it appears. For example we could have the sentence network (labelled S) contain an arc labelled S as in Fig 3.12.

S:

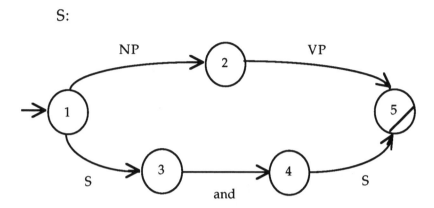

Fig 3.12 A recursive transition network

Note there is a route through the network which avoids the label **S**. If there had not been there would have been an infinite loop, forever sending you back to the **S** network and never reaching the final state, state 5.

This kind of network is called a **recursive transition network**. Clearly, just as we can have a recursive pair of rules in a context free grammar without either rule being recursive within itself, so too we can have recursion within the set of transition networks based on an interacting pair of networks, as in Fig 3.13.

Recursive transition networks are discussed more fully, and implemented in Prolog, in Gazdar and Mellish (1989).

We are beginning to see how recursive transition networks are equivalent to context free grammars. There are limitations with this style of grammar in handling natural language. One shortcoming is that it is not very easy to achieve agreement, such as that between the subject and verb of a sentence. For example, if the noun phrase that is the subject of a sentence is plural then we must use the plural form of the verb,

She smiles
They smile

It is a peculiarity of English that s, which indicates plural in nouns, also indicates third person singular in verbs.

NP:

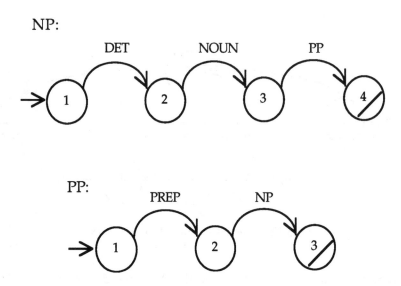

Fig 3.13 Recursion within a set of recursive transition networks

Another example is the feminine determiner *her*, which must be used with a feminine noun phrase:

> *John packed his own bag*
> *John's aunt packed her own bag*

It looks as if the unified treatment of all NPs as suggested by the network in Fig 3.13 is too simple. *Her own bag* is an NP of a particular kind that depends on the kind for *John's aunt.* We seem to be led into more and more subclassification of NPs. A more economical way to handle agreement is to have features attached to the words and phrases and a mechanism for ensuring that singulars go with singulars and plurals with plurals.

Different categories of word have different kinds of features attached to them in the lexicon. We say that there are different **dimensions** for the word categories. For example the dimensions for pronoun would include number (singular or plural), person (first, second or third), case (subjective, objective), gender (masculine, feminine or neuter). So we get

> *he* =   singular + third person + subjective + masculine
> *him* = singular + third person + objective + masculine
> *it* =   singular + third person + neuter
> { as *it* is both subjective + objective, they are omitted }

Exercise 3.8
There are various other dimensions that pronouns can have, including possessive (e.g. *his*) and reflexive (e.g. *himself*). If the pronoun is possessive we include the feature *+poss* and if it is not we include the feature *-poss*: similarly for reflexive (*+reflex* and *-reflex*). Using these, define the pronouns:

I, me, mine, myself, we, us, ourselves, themselves, their.

Verbs need a variety of features, including number and person. Thus *smiles* is the appropriate present tense form for third person singular while *smile* is the appropriate form for third person plural.

Augmented transition networks (ATNs) are able to accommodate such features. In addition to providing recursive transition networks they provide registers with each network, and conditions and actions that are associated with each arc. One kind of action is to assign a value to a register. A condition on traversing a later arc can test the value of such a register.

S:

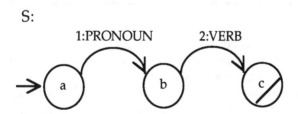

Register: **Number** = { singular, plural }

————————————————————————————

S1: Action:　　Set **Number** to number of Word
S2: Condition: Test **Number** = number of Word

————————————————————————————

Lexicon:

she	PRONOUN	(number = singular)
they	PRONOUN	(number = plural)
smiles	VERB	(number = singular)
smile	VERB	(number = plural)

Fig 3.14　Augmented transition network

In this extremely simplified ATN, **Word** is the variable that has as its value the current word being generated, complete with the set of features specified by the lexicon. The idea is that to traverse the first arc of this sentence network (S1) a word must be selected that is a **PRONOUN**. Then the **Number** register is set to the value of the **number** feature for that word. To traverse S2, a **VERB** must be selected which satisfies the condition that its value for **number** must be the same as the value in the **Number** register.

This is such a simple example that there would be little motive for handling the generation of those few sentences that way, but clearly the method comes into its own where there is more complexity. A number of registers would be required to keep the network down to manageable proportions. In a real example we would have a set of networks and the registers for **Person, Number** and **Gender** might be set while traversing the NP network and their values retained for use within the S network.

Exercise 3.9

Produce a transition network without augmentation that is equivalent to the ATN in Fig 3.14.

The notion of register used here is essentially the standard computer science notion of a special purpose memory location. Although this addition to the network structures may seem a sensible enhancement in order to deal more effectively with natural language phenomena, it should be appreciated that it involves moving closer to a computer programming approach and away from an abstract description of a grammar.

We are not able to deal with the details of operation of ATNs here. They were originally developed to deal with the problems of parsing using a transformational grammar, which will be described shortly. One linguistic phenomenon which provided an early motivation for the development of transformational grammar is passivization.

The corresponding passive form of

He boarded the Devon train.

is

The Devon train was boarded by him.

A context free grammar would generate those sentences quite independently (i.e. by quite separate rules) but they are semantically and also syntactically related.

ATNs can capture the commonality of underlying structure between active and corresponding passive sentences by establishing role registers including **Subject** (the subject in the active form), **Direct-Object, Main-Verb** and **Voice** (with the values *active* or *passive*).

3.6 Transformational grammar

As already mentioned in the previous section there is an approach to syntax which has been called **transformational grammar.** This is a form of generative grammar which significantly enhances the power of a context free grammar. It incorporates a context free grammar as a base but has in addition a different kind of rule, a transformational rule, that operates on the tree structures produced by the context free grammar.

The form of a transformational grammar has changed markedly over the years. We can get the spirit of the approach from the linguistic phenomena that provided the early motivations. Passivization has already been mentioned in connection with ATNs. The idea is that the structure of the active form is produced by the context free grammar. Then a passive transformation changes the structure to produce the corresponding passive form. The passive transformation has been written in this style,

   NP1 - V - NP2 => NP2 - is - V-EN - by - NP1

For example,

   John boards the Devon train => The Devon train is boarded by John

Where *boarded* is the past participle form (**V-EN**) of *boards*.

Note that **NP1** and **NP2** refer to the subject and direct object of the active structure, however complex they may be. The same rule would produce

   The last train to Devon is boarded by the man who broke the bank at Monte Carlo.

from

   The man who broke the bank at Monte Carlo boards the last train to Devon.

The passive transformation was just one of a number transformation rules that interacted in complex ways to produce a variety of natural language sentences.

Exercise 3.10

Consider how you would write a transformation rule that takes simple affirmative present tense English sentences like *You like Devon*, and produces the corresponding yes/no question *Do you like Devon?* Think about what other parts of a grammar are relevant.

In early transformational grammar a transformational rule was important in handling the complexities of verb groups, involving passives amongst other things. Remember that the passive *is* and the aspectual *is* and *have* all affect the following verb in their own characteristic ways (producing the **V-EN**, **V-ING** and **V-EN** forms respectively). This can be achieved by having the context free grammar generate (*is* -EN) for the passive, (*is* -ING) for the continuous aspect and *have* -EN for the perfect aspect. Then an **affix hopping** transformation moves the -EN and -ING affixes to after the next verb. Rules of morphology can then be used to produce the correct form, either a **V-EN** or a **V-ING**.

What has survived in transformational grammar over the years has not been such details as the affix hopping transformation or even the passive transformation but rather the general technique of having a more powerful kind of rule to transform structures produced by a context free grammar.

In the phrase structure component of Chomsky's (1957) original model, a context free grammar only generated the structures for simple, active, affirmative, declarative sentences (SAAD sentences), such as

SAAD sentence: *He packed his bags.*

Other types of sentence, such as

complex sentence: *He packed his bags and ran to the bus stop.*
passive sentence: *His bags were packed by himself.*
negative sentence: *He did not pack his bags.*
interrogative sentence: *Did he pack his bags?*
imperative sentence: *Pack his bags!*

are all generated using transformations. Actually, some transformations, such as the affix hopping one, are obligatory (though would have no affect if there are no affixes to hop). The SAAD sentences, which have only employed the obligatory transformations, are called **kernel sentences**.

The first main break with that model came in the 1960s with the publication of work by various of Chomsky's associates, but most notably Chomsky's own *Aspects of a Theory of Syntax* (1965). The approach adopted there came to be known as the **standard theory**. One of the main innovations in that model was that the phrase structure component included recursion, just as our context free grammar does, permitting the generation of complex sentences directly rather than by transformation. Also special symbols for negation, question and passive appeared in the phrase structure component. The appropriate transformations were now obligatory and would perform their changes just when those markers were present. One important result of these changes was that transformations no longer altered meaning.

These changes allowed the notion of **deep structure** to be introduced. The deep structure of a sentence is the phrase marker produced by the base component. The **surface structure** is derived by transformation. The notion of the deep structure of a sentence was not defined in the early system. One reason was that a complex sentence was not derived transformationally from a single phrase marker in the base but from several phrase markers, so there could be no one thing that was the deep structure in the early system.

Probably what generated most excitement for the standard theory notion of deep structure at the time was that it was the syntactic level that was semantically relevant. The deep structure was sometimes viewed, perhaps in a confused way, as being the fundamental structure of the sentence (directly representing the meaning), with the surface structure being the more superficial structure of the spoken or written form.

In Fig 3.15 two sentences are shown that are transformationally derived from similar deep structures.

Another innovation in the standard theory is that instead of lexical items being directly generated in the base a set of features is generated, leaving it to a lexical insertion rule to substitute a word of an appropriate kind. For example, the features

{[+Human] [+Common]}

might be generated and the lexical insertion rule may insert

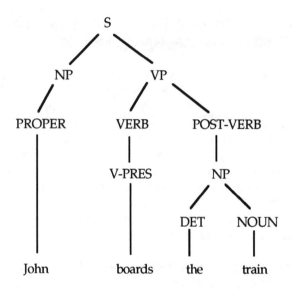

(a) Deep structure of *John boards the train*

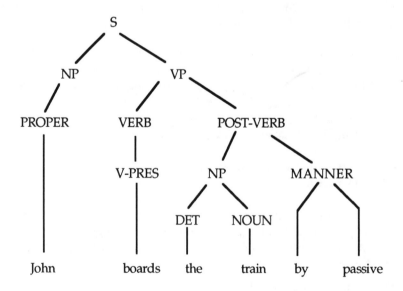

(b) Deep structure of *The train is boarded by John*

Fig 3.15 Active and passive sentences derived from similar deep structures

boy

This allows selectional restriction to be performed so that a verb such as *cancel* can only be used to generate sentences with a subject NP containing the feature [+Human] (see Section 5.2 for more details).

The use of transformational rules has proved extremely versatile in handling a broad range of linguistic phenomena. For example, the phenomenon of gapping, previously described, was readily described in the transformational framework. The complete non-elliptical form is generated in the base component and then a transformational rule can check for a duplication of a certain kind and delete the second occurrence. A specification of the conditions under which that can occur may involve some difficulties, however.

In the most recent form of transformational grammar, **government and binding**, there is just one transformational rule, a movement rule. The theory involves the interaction of various subsystems of principles putting constraints on what are well formed structures. Two of those subsystems are, unsurprisingly, government and binding.

Government concerns the relationship between the head of a construction and the categories dependent on it. For example, a verb governs phrases within its own verb phrase, but government does not extend to constituents of these phrases.

Binding concerns phrases being required to have the same reference; for example *John* and *himself* have the same reference in *John believes himself to be late*. For more about government and binding see Chomsky (1982).

In general, concerns about transformational grammar as a general approach have not been that it cannot handle certain phenomena but rather that the approach is so powerful that the challenge is to find principled restrictions to the form of a transformational grammar.

3.7 Case grammar

Transformational grammar, in various forms, has been the dominant paradigm in linguistics for some thirty years. However there have been various rival approaches still within the broad framework of generative grammar. One such approach is **case grammar**.

Applying the notion of case to a language such as English was frequently criticized in the early decades of scientific linguistics. This was because traditional grammar took the explicit case structure of inflected languages such as classical Greek and Latin and applied them without significant empirical justification to English, which lacks those inflections. Students of Latin learn that the noun for *table* comes with certain suffixes indicating various cases.

case	singular	plural
nominative:	*mensa*	*mensae*
vocative:	*mensa*	*mensae*
accusative:	*mensam*	*mensas*
genitive:	*mensae*	*mensarum*
dative:	*mensae*	*mensis*
ablative:	*mensa*	*mensis*

The nominative form is employed for the subject of a sentence and the accusative form is employed for the direct object. The word for *girl, puella,* follows a similar pattern. Thus we have

   Puella mensam vidit. (The girl saw the table)

The usage of some case forms is not so simple to specify in English. In Latin the use of inflections allows word order to be much freer than in English. Hence the following means the same

   Mensam puella vidit. (The girl saw the table)

'ome linguists would insist that the notion of case only applies to inflected ınguages such as Latin. But proponents of case grammar, notably Charles llmore (1968), think it wrong for the morphology to determine the syntactic ıtegories. Rather the categories must be responsive to the needs of the ᴍ̩ntax. Fillmore notes that there are different case structures to be found in ι̇ɪe surface structure of different languages and that they are indicated in various ways. But he argues that there is a relatively small set of basic cases that appear in the deep structures of all languages.

In transformational grammar it is easy to identify the subject of a simple sentence in deep structure. It is the NP in the NP VP immediately dominated by the S in the phrase marker. This could still be the subject in surface structure, but might alternatively be the indirect object following *by* in a passivized form. Case grammar maintains the spirit of the idea that a noun phrase has a certain place in deep structure that might be reflected in a variety of positions in surface structure. But that place is no longer identified as a position in a tree diagram, but rather is seen as a thematic role that has semantic significance (see Section 5.6).

Thus there is no notion of subject in deep structure, but there is the notion of **Agentive**, representing the animate individual that performed an action. The **Instrumental** case is exhibited by *a hammer* in both of the following

A hammer broke the window.
John broke the window with a hammer.

In the second sentence *John* has the case **Agentive** and thus shows up as the surface subject of that verb. But in the absence of a value for **Agentive** the **Instrumental** shows up as the surface subject.

A given verb has specified in the lexicon the range of cases it can take. Fillmore originally proposed six cases: **Agentive, Instrumental, Objective, Dative, Factive** and **Ablative,** but other proposals have been made. The general approach has been very influential in natural language processing and has stimulated the development of semantic networks (see Section 5.4) as an appropriate form of knowledge representation for natural language input and output.

3.8 Generalized phrase structure grammar

A current rival to transformational grammar involves revisiting phrase structure grammar and finding new resources to handle awkward syntactic phenomena. This version is called **generalized phrase structure grammar** (**GPSG**). In its early versions it can be shown to have had an equivalent generative capacity to a context free grammar. However it didn't specify context free rules directly, but indirectly by means of metarules, rules for generating rules. Later, as in Gazdar, Klein, Pullum and Sag (1985), there became less emphasis on metarules and there are no longer even indirectly specified context free grammar rules. Rather there are rules that directly specify the well formedness of trees.

One kind of rule is an immediate dominance (ID) rule which specifies which node can dominate which other nodes in a tree, but without the dominated nodes being ordered, as they are in a left to right fashion in a phrase structure tree diagram. They are written like this:

S -> NP, VP (which is equivalent to: S -> VP, NP).

Then there are linear precedence rules which precisely do govern left to right ordering among sister nodes all dominated by a single mother node. These apply throughout the grammar, in the sense of applying to each group of sister nodes in any tree. For example, a linear precedence rule might specify that Vs precede NPs which precede VPs whenever they are sisters. It is written thus:

V < NP < VP

Such a generalization would not be directly statable in a context free grammar, even if it held true for that grammar.

Metarules still have a place in GPSG. For example, one allows the generation of English passive verb phrases:

VP -> X, NP   =>   VP[PAS] -> X, (PP[by])

This states that where there is an ID rule in which a **VP** immediately dominates some other material together with an **NP** (the direct object), then a new rule can be created in which **VP[PAS]** immediately dominates that material without the direct object (for passives do not have direct objects) plus an optional *by*-phrase (the passive indirect object).

Categories in GPSG are strictly sets of features, although the familiar labels are used in the above examples of rules. Various rules specify how features are inherited.

3.9 Summary

We started this chapter by looking at the ways that words combine into phrases and sentences through the medium of a context free grammar. This took us into many different constructs in English that could well have comprised an entire book or more. That very complexity gives rise to the question of whether the way we have chosen to express grammar is appropriate.

Whilst those involved in natural language processing have tended to use context free grammars (probably because they understand their use in programming languages), pure linguists have been far more influenced by transformational grammar, which has appeared in several different versions over the past thirty years. Other forms of grammar have been proposed, such as case grammar and generalised phrase structure grammar and we could have mentioned several more.

Tree-adjoining grammar (Joshi et al, 1975) is one example which consists of rules for joining together simple phrase structure trees to form larger phrase structure trees. Certain features of natural language, such as number or gender agreement, can be stated simply within the simple trees and the tree-adjoining process can handle the awkward dependencies that can arise in some complex sentences.

It is a strange comment upon the research into processing natural language by computers that the speech processing researchers use a different approach from the text processing researchers, and the pure linguists use a different approach from the computational linguists. Whilst transformational grammar is the dominant paradigm within linguistics, there are few natural language text analysis systems that have even attempted to use it. In the next chapter, therefore, we will look at how we implement a context free grammar in Prolog so that we can analyse incoming sentences to tell whether they are grammatical and, if so, what their structure is. Later in Chapter 4 and in Chapter 5 we shall look at implementation of other types of grammar.

4

Parsing

4.1 The operations of a simple parser

In the previous chapter we developed a context free grammar adequate to describe the sentences found in our sample story. The full grammar is described in Fig 3.3 and the associated lexicon, which gives the word class or classes to which each word belongs, is given in Fig 3.4. Given such a grammar and lexicon it should be possible to write a computer program to determine whether or not any given text is constructed according to the rules of the grammar. If a sentence is grammatical then the program should also be able to describe its structure. If a sentence is ambiguous then the program should be able to describe all its possible structures. A program that performs such functions is called a **parser**. There are many different ways to construct a parser and the design may affect both its success and its efficiency. Different types of grammar also give rise to different types of parser; for example a transformational grammar gives rise to a very different type of parser from a context free grammar.

Let us start by considering a simple parser for our context free grammar in Fig 3.3. Each text that we present for analysis is represented as a list of words, so the first sentence is represented as a list of seven words.

[John, woke, to, the, sound, of, birds]

We wish our parser to tell us whether this text forms a valid sentence, denoted in our grammar by the symbol **S**. To do this it will examine all the rules that have an **S** on the left hand side, i.e. rules 1 to 3 inclusive.

Doing things methodically, our parser will first test whether the whole text matches the pattern on the right hand side of Rule 1 (i.e. **NP VP**) leaving nothing unprocessed. In order to attempt this match the parser will next look for rules with **NP** on their left hand side so that it can try to apply their patterns to the beginning of the text. This time it will not worry if the pattern does not match the whole text as the remainder can be tested to see if it is a **VP**. Having identified rules 4 to 7, the parser will start with Rule 4.

    4.   NP ::= PRONOUN

There are no rules which have **PRONOUN** on the left hand side, but there are entries in the lexicon for **PRONOUN**.

    PRONOUN ::= he | him | it | she | them

As the first word in the string, *John*, does not appear in this list it is not a valid **PRONOUN**, so Rule 4 cannot be applied.

Having reached a failure the parser does not give up but backtracks to the point where there are alternatives to be tried. Having failed on Rule 4, it will next try Rule 5

    5. NP ::=   PROPER

Again, there are no rules with **PROPER** on the left hand side, but there are entries in the lexicon.

    PROPER ::= Devon | John

This time the first word in the string does match, so the parser can record a success at identifying an **NP** at the start of the sentence. This success leaves the remainder of the sentence,

    [woke, to, the, sound, of, birds]

to be tested to see if it is a **VP**. We will not go through how it does this in detail but recommend it as a good exercise for readers who are not familiar with the operations of parsers.

Rule 1 is thereby identified as leading to a valid match and, if results were kept, it would be possible to describe the structure of the sentence that led to this conclusion. This is shown in Fig 4.1.

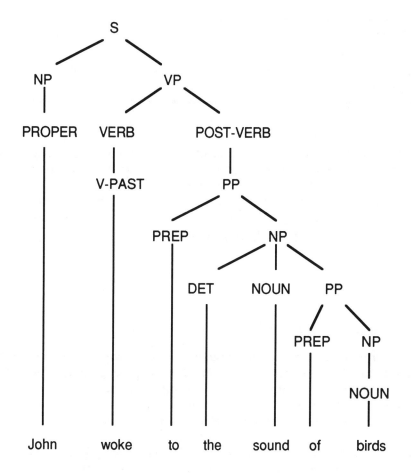

```
S ( NP ( PROPER = John )
    VP ( VERB ( V-PAST = woke )
         POST-VERB
              ( PP ( PREP = to
                    NP ( DET = the
                         NOUN = sound
                         PP ( PREP = of
                              NP ( NOUN = birds ) ) ) ) ) ) )
```

Fig 4.1 The structure of a valid sentence represented as
a tree and as a list structure

Exercise 4.1

Follow the operations of the parser in determining that the remaining
text, *woke to the sound of birds* , is a VP, keeping a log of the rules
applied.

Having found one successful description of the sentence the task is not
complete. The parser has to continue searching for any other possible
structures, as the sentence may be ambiguous. It has to explore Rules 6, 7 and 8
before going on to explore Rules 2 and 3. Only then can it conclude that this
analysis of the sentence is the only valid one according to this grammar, as it
will have explored all possible applications of the rules.

4.2 Getting the parser onto the computer

Section 4.1 gives an informal description of how a computer program to parse
sentences might work but it does not provide a computer program. You may feel
like taking this description and writing a parser in your favourite
programming language. If you do so then you will find that it will quickly
develop into a medium sized program of some complexity.

If you are familiar with the programming language Prolog you can take a short
cut, for that language has a special notation for defining context free grammars
and parsing them in the way we have described above (Clocksin & Mellish,
1981).   This notation is known as definite clause grammar (DCG).
Superficially, DCG rules are not very different from the description of context
free grammars we have given so far in this book. Fig 4.2 shows the first two
rules and their Prolog equivalents.

	Grammar Rules		Prolog
1.	S ::=	NP VP |	s --> np, vp.
2.		NVP VP	s --> nvp, vp.

Fig 4.2 Grammar rules coded in Prolog

The superficial differences between the two formulations are,

(a)   Prolog names must begin with a lower case letter. (* see below)

(b)   Only letters, numbers and the underscore character (_) may appear in Prolog names. (* see below)

(c)   The symbol '::=' becomes '-->' in Prolog.

(d)   Terms on the right hand side in Prolog are separated by commas.

(e)   Prolog rules are terminated by a full-stop.

(*   This is not strictly true as there are cases where you cannot avoid using an upper case letter at the beginning, for example, to represent the word *John* or *Devon*. Prolog does allow you to do this but you must enclose the word in single quotation marks every time you use it, e.g.
          proper --> ['John'].   )

There are some other differences which are more significant.

1.   The alternative symbol (|) is represented by rewriting the left hand side in full on each line. So, the first two lines of the grammar become, in Prolog,

        s --> np, vp.
        s --> nvp, vp.

2.   No predefined symbols in Prolog correspond to the optional symbol ([..]). It is represented by defining a new category that has two alternatives: those of being present or absent. (Absence in Prolog is represented by the empty list, [ ].) So a rule which states

        NP ::= [DET] NOUN

     becomes in Prolog

        np --> poss_det, noun.

        poss_det --> det.
        poss_det --> [ ].

     or

        np --> det ; [ ].

3.   No predefined symbol in Prolog corresponds to the repetition symbol (*). This symbol means *zero or more occurrences of* and can be represented in Prolog by allowing a recursive call in the definition of the repeated term.

So a rule that says

6.   NP ::= ADJ* NOUN

becomes in Prolog

np --> adjs, noun.

adjs --> adj, adjs.
adjs --> [ ].

4.   Items in the lexicon contain the words of the language on their right hand side. Each word can be represented in Prolog as a list of one item. For example,

pronoun --> [it].
pronoun --> [she].

All the items in the lexicon are handled this way, including the case of **ADJ** where there is a mixture of types of definition:

ADJ ::= V-EN | V-ING | first | full | fun | green

which becomes in Prolog

adj --> v_en.
adj --> v_ing.
adj --> [first].
adj --> [full].
adj --> [fun].
adj --> [green].

5.   The final major difference concerns recursive rules. The simplest examples of recursive rules are those in which the symbol on the left hand side is also used on the right hand side. Rule 7 is a recursive rule as it uses the symbol **NP** on both sides,

7. NP ::= QU-PH NP

In this rule the term that is used recursively (**NP**) appears on the right hand side after a term which must be present (**QUANT-PH**). This type of recursion causes no particular problem for our Prolog parser. Rule 3 is also recursive but it is different:

3. S ::= S CONJ S

This is a problem because the term that is used recursively (S) appears as the first term on the left hand side of the rule (this is known as left recursion). It is tempting, but quite wrong, to code Rule 3 in Prolog as

s --> s, conj, s.   % never do this

The reason why you should never do this becomes apparent when you consider how the parser operates. Given any sentence the parser will in time explore Rules 1 to 3. When it comes to apply Rule 3 it tries to match the pattern S CONJ S against the whole sentence. To do this it finds those rules with S on the left hand side (i.e. Rules 1 to 3). When it comes to apply Rule 3 again it tries to match the pattern, S CONJ S, against the whole sentence once more.

It should be clear that the parser has got itself into an endless loop testing whether the text commences with an S by testing whether the text commences with an S. From this the only escape will be when the computer's resources are exhausted.

The reason for this loop is that we have not insisted that some part of the sentence is consumed before the recursive call takes effect. If we insist on this then progress will be made and what is presented to the rule each time will be different from its predecessor. If no such commitment is made then, at some point, the parser will loop endlessly.

The outcome of this is that Prolog grammar rules cannot handle left recursion. It is not something that will produce a syntax error but if the system is confronted by left recursion then an endless loop will result at run-time. It is therefore up to the programmer to avoid left recursion in programs.

We can achieve this by defining something called a *simple sentence,* which is defined in Rules 1 and 2.

SIMPLE-S ::=   NP VP |
                  NVP VP

We can now say that a proper sentence is either a simple sentence or a compound sentence:

S ::=   SIMPLE-S |
         SIMPLE-S CONJ S

This way we have avoided left recursion, as in our reformulation what occurs before the CONJ S must satisfy one of the first two rules, i.e. it must be either NP VP or NVP VP.

These two rules very nearly express what we wanted to say in Rule 3 and can be coded safely in Prolog as they do not contain left recursion. The only limitation of this technique is that we are only able to represent a multiple compound in terms of the structure,

SIMPLE-S CONJ (SIMPLE-S CONJ SIMPLE-S)

and we are unable to represent multiple compound structures of the form

(SIMPLE-S CONJ SIMPLE-S) CONJ SIMPLE-S.

In practice there are not many occasions where we would want to do this, but some do occur. For example,

John will be disappointed and his mother will be worried unless his aunt has phoned her.

could be interpreted as,

(John will be disappointed and his mother will be worried) unless his aunt has phoned her.

or,

John will be disappointed and (his mother will be worried unless his aunt has phoned her).

The second of these interpretations can be captured by the coding we suggest, but the former cannot.

Accepting this limitation, the full Prolog coding for the category S becomes

```
s --> simple_s.
s --> simple_s, conj, s.

simple_s --> np, vp.
simple_s --> nvp, vp.
```

Similar techniques need to applied to code Rules 8 and 17.

The full Prolog equivalent of the grammar in Fig 3.3 is given in Fig 4.3. and the Prolog equivalent of part of the lexicon is given in Fig 4.4.

Exercise 4.2

Rewrite the left recursive rules 8 and 17 in the original grammar so that they are no longer left recursive.

```
s --> simple_s.
s --> simple_s, conj, s.

simple_s --> np, vp.
simple_s --> nvp, vp.

np --> simple_np.
np --> simple_np, [and], np.

simple_np --> pronoun.
simple_np --> proper.
simple_np --> poss_det, adjs, clasfs, noun, pps, poss_rel_cl.
simple_np --> poss_quph, np.

poss_det --> det ; [ ].

adjs --> adj, adjs.
adjs --> [ ].

clasfs --> clasf, clasfs.
clasfs --> [ ].

clasf --> noun ; proper.

pps --> pp, pps.
pps --> [ ].

pp --> prep(P), np.

poss_rel_cl --> rel_cl ; [ ].

rel_cl --> rel_pron, vp.

quph --> quant, [of].

nvp --> v_ing, post_verb.

vp --> simple_vp.
vp --> simple_vp, [and], vp.

simple_vp --> poss_modal, poss_have, be, poss_advb, adj.
simple_vp --> poss_modal, poss_have, poss_be, poss_advb, verb,
          post_verb.
```

```
poss_modal --> modal.
poss_modal --> modal, [not].
poss_modal --> [ ].

poss_have --> have ; [ ].

poss_be --> be ; [ ].

poss_advb --> adverb ; [ ].

post_verb --> poss_advb, poss_np, pps, poss_v_mod.

poss_np --> np ; [ ].

poss_v_mod --> poss_to_ph.
poss_v_mod --> rel_pron, s.
poss_v_mod --> [ ].

poss_to_ph --> [to], v_inf, post_verb ; [ ].
```

Fig 4.3 The grammar expressed in Prolog

```
det --> [a].
adj --> [full].
noun --> [sound].
proper --> ['John'].                    % quotation marks needed
pronoun --> [them].
prep --> [in].
rel_pron --> [who].
conj --> [and].
be --> [am].
have --> [has].
v_inf --> [sound].
v_pres --> [trains].
v_past --> [left].
v_en --> [broken].
v_ing --> [going].
adverb -> [immediately].
```

Fig 4.4 Part of the lexicon expressed in Prolog

Exercise 4.3

Not all prepositions can be associated with all verbs. For example, the verb *to go* might well be followed by the prepositions *in, down, through, past,* etc. but not by the preposition *of* . As none of the verbs in our story can take *of* , we can make our grammar more precise if that particular preposition is restricted to noun phrases. Implement this by amending the grammar and lexicon in Figs 4.3 and 4.4.

Having defined our grammar and lexicon to the Prolog system we can then apply it to a sample text by issuing the predefined command

phrase (s, ['John', woke, to, the, sound, of, birds]).

If the text we provide as the second argument is a grammatical sentence (i.e. an s) then the system will respond *yes*, otherwise it will respond *no*.

One can also use *phrase* to test any part of a sentence. For example,

phrase (np, [the, sound, of, birds]).

should succeed whereas

phrase (np, [to, the, sound, of, birds]).

should fail. The command *phrase* therefore provides us with a direct implementation of the test for grammaticality.

4.3 Restricting the application of rules

When discussing ATNs in Section 3.5 we noted that one way to make a grammar more precise without dramatically increasing the number of rules is to associate various features with words in the lexicon and to place restrictions on the way these features interact.

For example, both *train* and *trains* appear in Fig 4.4 as nouns with no distinction made between them:

noun --> [train].
noun --> [trains].

It is possible, within the Prolog formalism, to express features of nouns (or any other word class) by using arguments, as in

> noun(singular) --> [train].
> noun(plural) --> [trains].

This says that *train* is a singular noun whilst *trains* is a plural noun. A noun clause can then be made to adopt the features of its main noun by amending the rule as follows,

> np(X) --> poss_det, adjs, clasfs, noun(X), pps, poss_rel_cl.

In Prolog notation, terms beginning with capital letters (and not contained in quotation marks) function as variables whose scope is the particular clause within which they appear. We can introduce as many of these variables as we wish, giving them separate terms where they are to be distinct and repeating a term where we wish the values to be identical.

So a noun phrase that contains the word *train* as its main noun results in a match being established between

> noun(singular) --> [train].

and part of the right hand side of the rule,

> np(X) --> poss_det, adjs, clasfs, noun(X), pps, poss_rel_cl.

As a result of this match the variable X becomes instantiated to the value *singular*. This applies to the left hand side of the rule as well as the right, so we establish that we have found an **np(singular)**. A sentence that contained the word *trains* in the same place would be classified as **np(plural)**.

Verbs and verb phrases can be handled similarly. We could change the lexicon to read

> v_pres(singular) --> [runs].
> v_pres(plural) --> [run].

and adapt the rules

> verb(X) --> v_pres(X).
> . . .

> vp(Y) --> poss_have, poss_be, poss_advb, verb(Y), post_verb.

So a verb phrase that contains *runs* as its main verb will be classified as **vp(singular)** and one with *run* in the same place as **vp(plural)**.

Having made these two changes we can reconsider the first rule for a sentence, which we can adapt to read,

    s --> np(Z), vp(Z).

That is to say, we can now force the subject noun phrase to agree with the verb. This grammar will now allow sentences such as

    The train runs.
    The trains run on time.

but will not allow

    *   *The trains runs.*
    *   *The train run on time.*

Exercise 4.4

Develop a system of features to check that the determiner, if it is present, matches the head noun in a noun phrase. The system should allow *the train, the trains, trains* and *a train*, but not allow * *a trains*.

Exercise 4.5

The grammar in Fig 3.3 does not take into account verb tenses and this leads to some undesirable results. For example, it allows *be* as a main **VERB**, so that *can be* is analysed as (**NOUN** = can) and (**VERB** = be).

The permissible tenses in this restricted grammar are represented by the following rules

    A **modal** is to be followed by a **V-INF**.
    A **HAVE** auxiliary must be followed by a **V-EN**.
    A **BE** auxiliary must be followed by a **V-EN** or a **V-ING**.
    Otherwise, the verb must be **V-PAST** or **V-PRES**.

Implement these by adding appropriate arguments to the grammar and lexicon in Figs 4.3 and 4.4.

4.4 Describing the structure

The use of arguments in the previous section to check the compatibility of features can be extended to develop a description of the structure of valid sentences, such as the list shown in Fig 4.1. We will ignore the layout on the page and develop the basic structure of the representation, which is given by the two rules

(a)   Items retrieved from the lexicon: these are represented by the category, followed by an equals sign (=), followed by the word. For example,

proper = John

(b)   Items derived by grammar rules: these are represented by the category from the left hand side of the rule, followed by the representation of each of the categories on the right hand side, enclosed in round brackets. For example, an application of the first rule will result in

s (np (...), vp (...))

We implement these rules by creating a new variable in every rule which will contain the representation. For the lexicon we use the first of these rules, so we get

```
det(det = a) --> [a].
det(det = her) --> [her].
... etc.
```

(Note: In Prolog the symbol '=' is predefined as an infix operator, i.e. one that can appear between its arguments. The expression 'det = a' is therefore treated as a single object.)

For the grammar rules, we take the representations provided by the underlying categories and build a new representation, as in

pp(pp(P, N)) --> prep(P), np(N).

If we are already using one argument, as in

s --> np(Z), vp(Z).

we create a second, making sure we are consistent about the order in which they appear. So, we could have

s(s(X, Y)) --> np(X, Z), vp(Y, Z).

Where we are dealing with optional entries we insert the empty list where the option is not taken, as in

    poss_det(X) --> det(X).
    poss_det([ ]) --> [ ].

Repetition is handled by

    adjs([A | X]) --> adj(A), adjs(X).
    adjs([ ]) --> [ ].

which will build a list of representations of adjectives in the order in which they appear in the text.

Exercise 4.6

Amend the grammar rules and the lexicon to produce representations. The structure of a sentence may be obtained by typing

   phrase (s(R), [John, woke, to, the, sound, of, birds]).

This will check that the sentence is valid and, if it is, return a representation of its structure bound to the variable **R**. If it is not successful, nothing will be bound to **R** and if there are multiple possible interpretations these may be found by responding with a semi-colon in the normal way for Prolog.

This representation will not contain the new lines and tabs that are shown in Fig 4.1, and it will contain a number of empty lists where options are not taken up. This may make the representation slightly less easy to read, but will not affect the correctness of the result. Experienced Prolog programmers might like to write a routine to print the representation in a more attractive format.

4.5 Using charts

The algorithm described in Section 4.1 works by starting with the largest constituent of the text, the sentence (S), and seeing what immediate constituents it can have. It then repeats this process for each of these constituents, and so on until it finds words of the required part of speech. As it works from the largest constituent to the smallest, it is sometimes known as a

top-down approach to parsing.

It would be possible to build a parser that worked the other way, finding first the parts of speech of the words in the text, then seeing if they match the patterns on the right hand side of any rule. If so, it could establish that the constituent represented by the left hand side of that rule may be present. Eventually, such a procedure could establish that the S constituent is present, i.e. we have a valid sentence. Such an approach, working from the smallest constituents to the largest, is sometimes known as a **bottom-up** approach.

Pure top-down or bottom-up approaches can be inefficient. For example, the algorithm in Section 4.1 is very thorough but, because it explores each rule as if for the first time, duplicates a lot of work. In this simple parser the rules for a category are applied in the order in which they appear in the listing. The rules that define the category **simple-np**, for example, will always be explored in the sequence they appear in the listing even though they may have appeared in any order. In a system that exhaustively explores every possibility there are no gains to be obtained by using one order rather than another but if, for example, we were only interested in the first successful parse then it would be more efficient to place the more commonly used rules first.

Inefficiency occurs when the parser has to explore the same proposition a number of times. For example, every attempt to match s will result in using the first two rules,

s --> simple_s.
s --> simple_s, conj, s.

The process that searches for a **simple_s** will therefore be executed twice for every sentence.

The more options there are in a grammar the more chance there is that a parser will try to prove something that it has already tried before and thereby waste time. As any solution to this problem of inefficiency will have a cost associated with it, a small amount of duplication is not a serious problem. If the problem becomes acute then it can be avoided by recording the result of every attempted match. Whenever the parser is confronted by a match it will first search a table of results to see whether it has previously tried to make the same match (see Fig 4.5). If it has tried to make the match, the system can read the outcome of that previous attempt and determine immediately whether or not it was successful. If there has been no previous attempt then the parser will try to make the match using the method described in the previous section, recording the result when it has completed its attempt.

result(['John'], [np], yes).
result(['John'], [pronoun], no).
result([the,sound,of,birds], [np], yes).

Fig 4.5 One way of storing the results of attempts

This is not as simple to implement in Prolog as the basic parser. It requires writing another version of the basic *phrase* routine and only experienced Prolog programmers should try to do so. With parsers written in other languages the changes may be easier. Significant improvements can be obtained with some grammars using this technique, though the details will depend upon the language used and the implementation.

The technique of storing the results of attempted parses has been developed into a special technique known as **chart parsing.** In a chart parser there are two lists which are used to indicate the state of the parse at any stage. One is the **inactive list**, which is a list of those parts of the text which have been successfully identified. Initially it contains entries for each of the individual words in the sentence and records the lexical category of each as found in the lexicon. If a word appears more than once in the lexicon (as in the case of *sound* in Fig 4.6) then a separate entry is made in the inactive list for each category. The other list is the **active list**, which is a list of hypotheses about the possible structure of the text. Initially it contains separate entries for all of the possible definitions of S. For reasons we shall discuss later, left-recursion is not a problem for chart parsers.

I1:   inactive (proper, [proper], ['John']).
I2:   inactive (verb, [verb], [woke]).
I3:   inactive (prep, [prep], [to]).
I4:   inactive (det, [det], [the]).
I5:   inactive (noun, [noun], [sound]).
I6:   inactive (v_inf,[v_inf],[sound]).
I7:   inactive (prep, [prep], [of]).
I8:   inactive (noun, [noun], [birds]).

A1:   active (s, [ ], [np, vp], [ ], ['John', woke, to , the, sound, of, birds]).
A2:   active (s, [ ], [nvp, vp], [ ], ['John', woke, to , the, sound, of, birds]).
A3:   active (s, [ ], [s, conj, s], [ ], ['John', woke, to , the, sound, of, birds]).

Fig 4.6   The initial state of the chart parser

The first item on the active list (A1) has five arguments which represent

argument	meaning
s	we are trying to prove the structure is an **s**.
[]	we have not yet found any categories.
[np, vp]	we are trying to prove it is composed of **np, vp**.
[]	we have not yet identified any of the text.
['John', woke, to , the, sound, of, birds]	
	we have this text still to work with.

The basic strategy is to confirm the hypotheses on the active list by either matching them against items on the inactive list or expanding them by applying rules which define the first category of their third argument. When a hypothesis has been confirmed it is taken off the active list and put onto the inactive list. A successful parse has been found when an item appears on the inactive list of type **s** with no text left to work with. All parses have been found when there are no items on the active list that can be explored further.

In the example (Fig 4.6) there is nothing on the inactive list to help us confirm A1, so we must look for rules which define the first category of the third argument (i.e. rules which define **np**). This will generate more items on the active list.

A4:   active (np,[ ], [pronoun], [ ], ['John', woke, to, the, sound, of, birds]).

A5:   active (np,[ ], [proper], [ ], ['John', woke, to, the, sound, of, birds]).

A6:   active (np, [ ], [poss_det, adjs, clasfs, noun, pps, poss_rel_cl], [ ], ['John', woke, to, the, sound, of, birds]).

A7:   active (np, [ ], [quant, np], [ ], ['John', woke, to, the, sound, of, birds]).
A8:   active (np, [ ], [np, [and], np], [ ], ['John', woke, to, the, sound, of, birds]).

At some point the chart parser will recognise that the second of these active items (A5) can be matched to the first inactive item (I1), i.e.

A5:   active (np,[ ], [proper], [ ], ['John', woke, to , the, sound, of, birds]).

matches,

I1:   inactive (proper, [proper], ['John']).

The initial effect of this is to amend the active item to

A5:   active (np,[proper], [ ], ['John'], ['woke, to , the, sound, of, birds]).

The meaning of this is as follows,

argument	meaning
np	we are trying to find an **np**.
[proper]	we have found a **proper** which is at least part of what is required.
[]	nothing else is required.
['John']	this identification involves the text *John*.
[woke, to , the, sound, of, birds])	
	this text is not used in the identification.

This is only a temporary stage as the third argument indicates that nothing more is required, i.e. the item is no longer active.   Item A5 is therefore removed and replaced by an inactive item,

  I9:   inactive (np, [proper], ['John']).

This means that the text *John* has been found to be an **np** that consists of a single **proper**. This new inactive item will, in turn, lead to a change in A1 from

  A1:   active (s, [ ], [np, vp], [ ], ['John', woke, to , the, sound, of, birds]).

to

  A1:   active (s, [np], [vp], ['John'], [woke, to , the, sound, of, birds]).

The five arguments now represent

argument	meaning
s	we are trying to prove the structure is an **s**.
[np]	we have found the category **np**.
[vp]	we are trying to prove that is also has a **vp**.
['John']	we have identified the text *John* .
[woke, to , the, sound, of, birds]	
	we still have this text to work with.

This will lead to the creation of three new active items,

  A9:   active (vp, [ ], [poss_modal, poss_have, be, poss_advb, adj], [ ], [woke, to , the, sound, of, birds]).

  A10:   active (vp, [ ], [poss_modal, poss_have, poss_be, poss_adv, verb, post_verb], [ ], [woke, to , the, sound, of, birds]).

  A11:   active (vp, [ ], [vp, [and], vp], [ ], [woke, to , the, sound, of, birds]).

Eventually, after much processing which we will not explain in detail, item A10 will be confirmed and a new inactive item will be created,

   Ix: inactive (vp, [verb, post_verb], [woke, to, the, sound, of, birds]).

This records the fact that *woke to the sound of birds* is a **vp** consisting of a **verb** followed by a **post_verb**. By this time, of course, there will also be inactive items confirming that *to the sound of birds* is a **post_verb** and detailing all its components.

The new inactive item can now be combined with the active item

   A1:   active (s, [np], [vp], ['John'], [woke, to, the, sound, of, birds]).

to create

   Ay: active (s, [np, vp], [ ], ['John', woke, to, the, sound, of, birds], [ ]).

which becomes the inactive item

   Iz: inactive (s, [np, vp], ['John', woke, to, the, sound, of, birds]).

The creation of an inactive item of type s that refers to the entire text indicates that a successful parse has been found. Whilst we have described charts in terms of the operations on two lists, it is also possible to think of them diagrammatically. The state of the chart when it recognizes the first successful parse of the sentence is shown in Fig 4.7.

Unlike the parser in Section 4.1, the order in which rules (i.e. active items) are examined is not specified. To examine them in the same way as that parser, items would be added to the end of the active list and the bottom item would always be explored first. Other strategies can, however, be tried. For example, one could develop a breadth-first search of the grammar, as opposed to the depth-first searching in Section 4.1, or one could use heuristics to decide which active item to explore next.

If the parser decides to examine the third item,

   A3:   active (s, [ ], [s, conj, s], [ ], ['John', woke, to, the, sound, of, birds]).

it will look for ways to start the text with an s and this would generate the three items

   Aa: active (s, [ ], [np, vp], [ ], ['John', woke, to, the, sound, of, birds]).

   Ab: active (s, [ ], [nvp, vp], [ ], ['John', woke, to, the, sound, of, birds]).

   Ac: active (s, [ ], [s, conj, s], [ ], ['John', woke, to, the, sound, of, birds]).

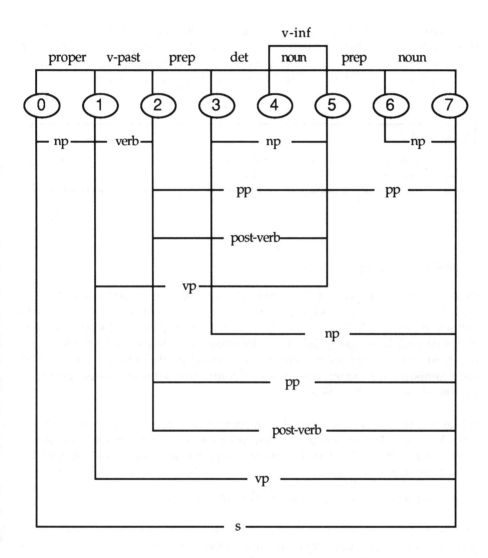

Fig 4.7 Chart parser after finding first successful parse

However, these items are identical to items A1, A2 and A3. If the chart parser does not add an item to a list if it is already there then the attempt to apply Rule 3 at this stage would result in no new items being created. The problem of left recursion has thereby been avoided.

Chart parsers are therefore important because they remember what they have tried so far which can make them more efficient, they deal naturally with left recursion, and they provide a formalism within which the problem of deciding the order in which to explore the various rules is left open.

Exercise 4.7

Show the state of the chart after it had explored all possible parses of the sentence.

4.6 Using expectations

One problem with parsers built around the idea of exhaustive searching is that they can take a very long time over lengthy sentences which have many options to explore. This does not often happen when humans process language. When natural language is spoken, rather than written, the person to whom it is addressed is required to process it incrementally, and to some extent deterministically, rather than waiting until the sentence ends and then looking for all possible parses.

It is also true that we are often able to compensate for missing words in a text (sometimes we do not even notice they are missing) and to complete a sentence with exactly the word that the speaker was intending to use. Consider the partial sentence,

On his way to the bus stop John called in at the ...

According to the grammar in Fig 3.3, any noun can be used as the head noun of this phrase, but it would be exceedingly odd to complete the sentence with nouns such as *tomato, cloud, completion* or *percentage*. There are a limited number of likely nouns, such as *bank, pub, chemist* etc. This is an example of prediction and it would be helpful if we could incorporate this ability in some way in our parser; it would reduce the number of options provided by a grammar and hence greatly speed up processing.

A straightforward way to do this is to hold predictions in the entries for words in the dictionary. This was the main idea behind a parser known as ELI (English Language Interpreter) built by Reisbeck (Schank & Riesbeck, 1981).

Each entry in the dictionary contained predictions in the form of a number of tests along with actions that were to be carried out when the test conditions were found to be true.

In order to fully appreciate the operations of such a predictive parser it must be realized that it is not intended to produce a parse tree as in Fig 4.1. The main theorist behind ELI, Roger Schank, argued that it is possible to go directly from the surface form of a sentence to a representation of its meaning (see Chapter 5). In ELI, the representation was in the form of conceptualizations (primitive verbs with their associated cases) plus a number of predicates (Schank & Colby,1973).

The second part of the sixth sentence in our story,

   S6b: *He ran to the bus stop.*

might be represented in this way as

   PTRANS (ACTOR = X1   OBJECT = X1   DIR-TO = bus-stop)
   male (X1)

Roughly translated, this means that we have a primitive act, **PTRANS** (referring to physical transfer), with some unknown object **X1** as its **ACTOR**, the same object **X1** as its **OBJECT** and **bus-stop** as its **DIRectional-TO** case. The **DIRectional-FROM** case is unknown and there is one predicate which states that **X1** is male. Had the sentence been

   John ran to the bus stop.

it would have been represented as

   PTRANS (ACTOR = John1 OBJECT = John1 DIR-TO = bus-stop)
            male(John1)

The parser that derives this structure is not complicated as the processing power is contained in the dictionary entries. The parser places a special symbol (traditionally **start**) on the front of the sentence to enable a stack and some predefined variables to be initialized, and then retrieves the definition of the next word from the dictionary, loads it onto the stack and executes the stack. Executing the stack consists of testing the top item to see if its conditions are met; if they are then the item is removed from the stack, its actions are executed and the stack is executed again. If the conditions of an item are not met then the definition of the next word is retrieved from the dictionary. If there are no more words and the stack is empty then processing has been successfully completed.

The definitions of words consist of tests that refer to a number of variables and actions that affect these variables or load new items onto the stack. The important variables and actions are described below.

Variable	Function
Word	the current word
Part_of_Speech	syntactic category of current word
CD_form	the output associated with the current object
Subject	the object that appears first
Concept	the resultant conceptualization for the whole sentence

Action	Function
assign_to(X,Y)	Assign the value of Y to the variable X. If Y is a variable, then the value of the variable is used.
add_to_stack(X)	The single argument, X, is loaded onto the stack.
assert(X)	The single argument, X, is added to the database (used for predicates).
get_var_name(X)	Generates a unique variable name.

The dictionary entries required for the analysis of the sample sentence are as follows.

```
*start*   assign_to (Part_of_Speech, nil)
          assign_to (CD_form, nil)
          add_to_stack
           ( if Part-of-Speech = np
             then assign_to (Subject, CD-form)
                  add_to_stack
                   ( if Part_of_Speech = verb
                     then assign_to (Concept, CD_form) ) )
```

Note: This will be activated before any of the text is read. It will cause the initialization of **Part_of_Speech** and **CD-form** and load the last five lines onto the stack. This sets up the basic strategy, which is to find an **np** and assign it to **Subject**, then find a **vp** and assign it to **Concept**.

```
bus stop   assign_to (Part_of_Speech, noun)
           assign_to (CD_form, bus_stop)
```

Note: The phrase is taken to be a **noun** and will appear as **bus_stop** in the final concept.

he   assign_to (Part_of_Speech, np)
get_var_name(X),
assign_to (CD_form, X)
assert (male (CD_form))

Note: The pronoun is taken to be an **np** and a variable is generated for its **CD_form**. It is asserted that this variable is **male**. The instructions in ***start*** will ensure that, in this example, this variable is also assigned to the variable **Subject**.

ran   assign_to (Part_of_Speech, verb)
assign_to (CD_form,
            ptrans(actor = V1, object = V1, to = V2, from = V3))
assign_to (V1, Subject)
add_to_stack
(if Word = to
  then add_to_stack
        (if Part_of_Speech = np
            then assign_to (V2, CD_form))
  else
  if   Word = home
  then   (assign_to (V2, CD_form)
              assert (house (CD_form))))

Note: Verbs have the most complicated definitions. The first four lines identify a verb and set up a **CD-form** based on the primitive act and its related cases. The contents of **Subject** are identified as being the **ACTOR** and **OBJECT** cases. The instructions in ***start*** will ensure that this structure is assigned to **Concept**. The last nine lines set up expectations for either the word *to* (i.e. *ran to ...*) or the word *home* (i.e. *ran home*). This is clearly an illustration of how complexity can be handled rather than a realistic account.

the   add_to_stack (if Part_of_Speech = noun
                then assign_to (Part_of_Speech, np))

Note: The word *the* awaits a following **noun** which it converts into an **np**.

to   { no entry }

Note: It is not necessary to have entries for every word in the dictionary, if they do not result in any changes then there is nothing to say about them. In this case the word is tested by an item on the stack, added by the definition of *ran*.

Exercise 4.8

Work through the steps of the expectation-driven parser, showing the contents of all of the variables, the database and the stack after each word of the sentence *He ran to the bus stop* has been processed.

The predictive parser gets away from the idea that all elements are of equal value in determining the structure of a sentence. We saw in the example how some words, especially verbs, do a lot of work whereas others, like the word *to*, do practically nothing. We can extend the idea of predictive parsing and process sentences by concentrating on the contexts in which we expect various words to appear and attaching to them specialist processes that actively seek out and structure the environment in which they appear. Parsers built around this idea are known as **word expert** parsers.

4.7 Deterministic parsing

It has already been noted that we digest phrases as they appear and even very long rambling sentences usually cause us no particular difficulty in comprehension. However, there are a few constructions in English which do cause us problems. For example, consider the way that in English we can take a sentence with a direct object and create a noun phrase from it, as in the following two examples.

the train left the station --> the station the train left
the man caught the train --> the train the man caught

We can quite happily combine the two sentences

the man caught the train and the train left the station

or

the man caught the train that left the station

but if we try to combine the noun phrases, using the same embedding techniques, we get

the station the train the man caught left.

This is bordering on the limits of intelligibility and if we were to do it once more,

the station the train the man the porter helped caught left

we have almost certainly hit overload. What is interesting is that if we sit down with pencil and paper we can disentangle this phrase and explain its structure and meaning. What does this show? It would seem to indicate that there are structures that are possible within the rules of a grammar but which are practically very difficult, if not impossible, to parse in real time. This may be evidence of how the human parser is constructed. (We have already mentioned in Section 3.4 how such difficulties are discussed by Chomsky in the study of performance.)

Further evidence as to the construction of the human parsing mechanism comes from what are known as **garden path sentences**. These are sentences which mislead us as to their correct syntactic structure and leave us in an impasse. The effect can be quite strong as we are usually unwilling to reconsider our earlier commitments. The following garden path sentences, for example, are both grammatical.

Have the soldiers given their medals by their sweethearts.
The boat sailed down the river sank.

In the first case we are dealing with an imperative, passive sentence whereas the natural assumption is that it is interrogative (as in *Have the soldiers given their medals to their sweethearts?*) . In the second we assume that *sailed* is the main verb (as in, *The boat sailed down the river.*) whereas the main verb is really *sank* and *sailed down the river* is a relative clause, as in ·
the boat that was sailed down the river.

Garden path sentences are fascinating but they are also informative. They seem to indicate that we make very firm commitments as to the syntactic structure of early parts of a sentence before we reach the end of the sentence and also that we are very reluctant to backtrack when we come to an impasse. Marcus (1980) explored this idea and designed a restricted machine that had two important features. By committing itself to syntactic structure as it processed left to right the time it took to process sentences was directly proportional to the length of the sentence. Secondly, it was able to reproduce the difficulties displayed by humans when faced by such phenomena as embedding and garden path sentences.

Though Marcus called his system a **deterministic parser**, it is easy to show that we cannot be totally deterministic when processing natural language (i.e. we cannot determine the correct category of every word and phrase as it appears). The two sentences,

> *Are the flowers in the vase?*
> *Are the flowers in the vase red?*

have radically different structures and which one applies becomes apparent only when processing proceeds past the word *vase*. There must therefore be some buffer area where we can keep words and phrases whose ultimate structural significance has yet to be decided. Marcus' claim was that this buffer could be restricted to three words or phrases.

So, if a deterministic parser were to process sentence 3, for example,

> S3: *Visiting aunts can be fun so he rang the station to discover the times of trains.*

it would initially load the first three words into its three buffer locations and then have to make some decisions as to their structure before the fourth word is seen. This does not seek to deny that the initial phrase in this sentence is ambiguous but only states that we do not maintain that ambiguity indefinitely. We are forced to opt for one interpretation rather than another and we do so at this precise stage rather than waiting until the end of the sentence.

Whichever way it is analysed, the phrase *visiting aunts* will be identified as a phrase which will be compressed into one item of the buffer. There is now room to read the fourth word, *be*. This will enable us to determine that *can* is functioning as a **modal** in this sentence and not as a **noun**. Making this judgement allows us another free space so that we can read the fifth word, and so processing continues.

It is often assumed that tackling a problem using computational techniques will be more efficient than tackling it by modelling human behaviour. The deterministic parser certainly questions this assumption. It also raises the question as to whether we should allow a system that generates text to apply all its rules without limit, for sometimes we may not be able to understand what it is saying, at least not without plenty of time and scrap paper.

4.8 Categorial grammar

One of the problems with both the predictive parser and the deterministic parser is that their definitions of language are too operational. That is to say they define a word in terms of the operations to be performed on some special type of machine and this type of definition has some serious weaknesses. Firstly it is not intuitively clear what is meant by the definition of a word in such a system and the justification for any particular definition is simply that it seems to work. Secondly, it can be very difficult to maintain and extend such parsers. Thirdly, they cannot be easily converted into devices that generate, rather than analyse, text according to a given grammar.

However, they do have their good points. The ability to process text from left to right in a relatively even manner, irrespective of the length of a sentence, is a definite plus and their ability to resolve ambiguity early gives them another strong advantage. Recently there has been a strong interest in linguistics in categorial grammars and the application of unification to grammars and parsing. One way of looking at these developments is to see them as ways of obtaining the advantages of these different types of parsers without the problems of an operational definition.

In **categorial grammars** most of the processing power is again kept in the dictionary by means of the categories that are associated with words. Typically there is a very small set of basic categories, usually represented by single letters (e.g. s, v, o). Other categories can be constructed out of these by means of a small number of connectives (e.g. the single connective / would enable the construction of such categories as s/v, $v/(o/o)$, etc). Each word is associated with one or more such categories in the lexicon.

As far as the parser is concerned, its only task is to implement the few rules that govern the combination of categories. Two such rules might be

$$R1: \quad X/Y + Y \rightarrow X$$
$$R2: \quad X/Y + Y/Z \rightarrow X/Z$$

R1 states that an object of category **X/Y** can combine with an object of category **Y** to its right and create a combined object of category **X**. R2 states that an object of category **X/Y** can combine with an object of category **Y/Z** to its right and create a combined object of category **X/Z**.

Assigning the following categories we can give a simple illustrative example:

John :	s/v	*runs* :	v
throws :	v/o	*sticks* :	o

The sentence *John runs* can then be analysed by the application of R1

```
John              runs
s/v               v
_____        : R1
        s
```

The sentence *John throws sticks* can be analysed by a double application of R1,

```
John            throws         sticks
s/v             v/o              o
                _____      : R1
                        v
_____        : R1
        s
```

or, alternatively, by the application of both rules

```
John            throws         sticks
s/v             v/o              o
_____                       : R2
        s/o
_____        : R1
        s
```

The implementation of these rules is an elementary operation, especially in a language such as Prolog in which such patterns may be expressed directly.

The categories of categorial grammar can be applied to any grouping of words in a sentence and are not restricted to the constituents of the sentence as defined by traditional grammars. This means that their application is not restricted to the traditional syntactic objects such as words, phrases and sentences. In Section 4.1 we analysed sentence 1,

S1: *John woke to the sound of birds.*

by identifying *to* as a **PREP**, *the* as a **DET**, *sound* as a **NOUN**, *the sound* as an NP and *to the sound* as a **PP**. What we could not do is describe the structure of the string *to the* for it is not a constituent in that grammar. Categorial grammars are not restricted in this way (and neither are expectation-based parsers) and it is possible to have descriptions of such phrases in terms of categorial structures.

4.9 Unification

Unification is essentially an abstract operation that will take two similarly structured objects and combine them into a single object. In our case the objects are standard descriptions of linguistic objects. If two descriptions are compatible then the result of unification will contain the features of both the contributing descriptions. If the two descriptions are incompatible in some way then the resulting description will be empty.

For example, the word *a* indicates that a noun phrase has been entered so it might create the object

    [cat = np,
       det = a,
       head = [cat = noun, number = singular]]

That is to say, it will expect a singular noun to form the head of the phrase. If the description for *locomotive* is

    [cat = noun,
       word = locomotive,
       number = singular]

This can be unified with the previous description to create

    [cat = np,
       det = a,
       head = [cat = noun, word = locomotive, number = singular]]

Whereas if the description for *locomotives* is

    [cat = noun,
       word = locomotive,
       number = plural]

This is incompatible with the previous description (as *number = singular* is incompatible with *number = plural*) so it will generate a null description (which is equivalent to failing).

A unification grammar is viewed as a description of all the possible sentences that can appear in the language. It will specify the objects that must exist, in terms of the features they must display and the order in which they must appear. It will typically contain many alternatives. Each word in a text can be unified with this grammar and acts as a restriction, eliminating certain options. The end of the sentence will usually eliminate further options and what is left is the description of the sentence. If it contains no alternatives then the sentence is unambiguous.

A unification grammar for our story could be based simply on our context free grammar, so the first three rules,

    1. S ::=   NP VP |
    2.   NVP VP |
    3.   S CONJ S

could be represented as

    {   [(np vp) cat = s]
        [(nvp vp) cat = s]
        [(s conj s) cat = s]}

In this notation the values in rounded brackets ('(...)') indicate the categories that must appear in the same order in the text. The curly brackets ('{ ... }') indicate a list of alternatives, each enclosed by square brackets ('[...]'). Similarly, the definition of **np** will start

    {   [(pronoun) cat = np]
        [(proper) cat = np]
        ... etc

For example, consider the sentence *He woke*. The parser will identify the first word in the sentence (*he*) as a **pronoun**, according to the definition

    def(he, [cat = pronoun,
                    gender = male,
                    number = singular,
                    person = 3,
                    word = he]).

and will unify this with the definition of **np** to create the object

    np = [cat = pronoun,
             gender = male,
             number = singular,
             person = 3,
             word = he]

It will then unify this with the definition of **s** to create the object

```
{[   (np vp)
        cat = s
        np = [    cat = pronoun,
                  gender = male,
                  number = singular,
                  person = 3,
                  word = he ] ]
 [   (s conj s)
        cat = s
        np = [    cat = pronoun,
                  gender = male,
                  number = singular,
                  person = 3,
                  word = he ] ]    }
```

At this stage it can eliminate one possible sentence structure, corresponding to rule 2, but it must allow for a possible conjunction. The processing of the word *woke* would result in its definition,

```
def( woke, [   cat = verb,
               tense = past,
               word = wake ] ).
```

creating the **vp** structure

```
vp =   [ cat = verb,
         tense = past,
         word = wake ]
```

This will be unified with the existing partial description of the sentence to create

```
{[  (np vp)
     cat = s
     np = [    cat = pronoun,
               gender = male,
               number = singular,
               person = 3,
               word = he ]
     vp = [    cat = verb,
               tense = past,
               word = wake ] ]
```

This is the result and, as can be seen, it contains a lot more information than the syntactic structure of our grammar in Section 4.1. There is clearly much more to unification grammars than we have been able to describe here. One issue to be resolved is the kind of description that should be given to objects, particularly whether it should be syntactic or functional. Different types of unification grammar, lexical unification grammar, functional unification grammar and unification categorial grammar tend to differ on their approach to this issue. Then, depending upon the approach to the issue of which features to represent, there is different scope for writing grammar rules. Finally, the order in which possible unifications are explored has to be decided as this effects the success and efficiency of parsing.

4.10 Summary

In this chapter we have looked specifically at how we might get a computer to do parsing. We started by using standard computational techniques and, in many situations, this may be sufficient. However, the desire to improve performance has led to an interest in human parsing processes and a number of parsers have been developed that try to mimic aspects of human performance. More recently, in categorial and unification grammars, we are seeing a return to more formal methods whilst retaining some of the advantages of human oriented devices.

5

Semantics

5.1 What do we mean by semantics ?

It is easy to say that when we are concerned with semantics we are concerned with meaning but what precisely is a meaning? That is a leading question which has no simple answer but let us consider some of the problems that we face in trying to answer it.

(a) Different kinds of linguistic object can have a meaning. Morphemes, words, phrases, sentences, utterances and stories can each be said to have a meaning but it is not necessarily the same thing in each case. The answer to the question *What is the meaning of the morpheme -ing?*, for example, might be a very different kind of thing from the answer to the question *What is the meaning of the story you have just read?*

(b) In natural language some words have more than one meaning (e.g. *can, post, go*) but how do we know where one meaning ends and the next begins? How many meanings of the verb *to go* are there in

> *to go home*
> *to go crazy*
> *to go off the boil*
> *to go absent*
> *to go ape*
> *to go slow*
> *to go away* ?

(c)   Do we ever break out of the endless circle of defining words in terms of other words ? If we define

a bachelor is a man who has never married

that gives us the meaning of *bachelor*, but what is the meaning of *a man who has never married* ?

These and other problems make the approach to natural language semantics rather daunting, but it need not be. We can begin with something relatively simple: the semantics of artificial languages such as programming languages.

In the case of a high-level programming language we can find one type of semantics represented by its compiler.   The purpose of the compiler is to produce a set of operations which have the same intent as the instructions written in the high-level language but which can be executed on a given computer. For a given program compiled by, say, a Pascal compiler for an IBM PC we can say that the meaning of the program is the machine code produced by the compiler. Of course this is a special case and there are difficulties if we try to generalize from this example (the semantics of a program, for example, cannot tie it to any particular machine code) but we at least have found some foundation upon which we can build a system of semantics.

As Woods (1978) has pointed out, there are three parts to a semantic definition such as this.

(a)   A meaning representation language (MRL), which is a notation in which to represent meanings.
(b)   A specification of what the MRL means.
(c)   An interpretation procedure to convert statements in the original language into the corresponding MRL notation.

In the example of the Pascal compiler for an IBM PC these three parts correspond as follows.

(a)   The MRL is the machine code of the IBM PC.
(b)   The meaning of the MRL is the effect of these operations on the PC (which is independently defined).
(c)   The interpretation procedure is the transformation carried out by the Pascal compiler.

When using this approach to semantics for natural language there are many possibilities for an MRL. Whether some formalism (a logic, for example) is chosen or whether a new formalism is created it should ideally meet four criteria.

1. It should provide distinct representations for all the different meanings that any string of words may have (e.g. if a sentence has four possible interpretations then we expect them to match four different representations in the MRL).

2. It should provide a single representation if two different strings of words have the same meaning (e.g. *John boarded the Devon train* and *The Devon train was boarded by John* should have very similar or identical representations).

3. It should be complete (anything that can be meaningfully said in the original language should be able to be represented in the MRL).

4. It should be sound (it should not be possible to construct a representation that does not have a corresponding meaning expressible in the original language).

Beyond this our guiding principle is that semantics is closely related to purpose. If you want to represent the meaning of something then find out what the system is supposed to do and ensure that the representation is adequate to enable that purpose to be achieved.

If there is a distinction to be drawn between computational linguists and those working in natural language processing it is most likely to be found in their attitude towards semantics. The field of natural language understanding tends to be concerned with semantics in relation to the human use of machines and this use normally has quite specific objectives. Natural language processing may be required in a variety of computerized systems (e.g. database access, machine translation, the automatic production of indexes or abstracts and question answering). In general, the semantics will be directed towards the objectives of the system and they are easier to define than in the more general case of unrestricted natural language.

An example of such a system is a front-end to a database, in which the objective will be to transform any valid natural language input into a corresponding expression that can be used to access the database. The MRL could be a standard database access language (e.g. SQL) which has the advantage that its meaning is defined independently. The interpretation procedure will be the transformation between natural language input and its SQL equivalent.

In many cases, however, there will not be a ready-made formal notation, such as machine code or SQL, with an acceptable semantics available to us. We will then have to design a semantics that is both representationally adequate and has a definable meaning. This is where the objective of the system becomes relevant, for if the system is to perform inferences, for example, then the representational form must not only be descriptively adequate but it must have its own semantics which permit legal inferences to take place in a way that is both consistent and complete.

Many practical systems have been able to successfully represent meaning within their system, but such success brings with it a potential cost. It could be argued that the difficult problem of natural language semantics has been solved in such systems by treating natural language as if it were artificial. The danger in this is that there may be meaningful things that we can say in natural language that will not be understandable in the semantics proposed. To give an example, we might be able to use a front-end to a financial database to ask *What is the price of BP shares?* but the system would not be able to understand *Is it time for my coffee break?* If this is true then in what sense can we claim to be processing natural language?

The computational linguist tends to see language in its more general context and so relates meaning to its role in communication between human speakers of the language. These speakers are autonomous agents with a multitude of hopes, values and purposes and the problem of devising a system of semantics capable of capturing all the complexities of the human use of language to convey meaning has proved to be very hard indeed.

Traditionally in linguistics the problem of representing meaning is broken down into stages. The first stage is concerned with what we might call the literal meaning of things. Many strings of words which seem to have no literal meaning can be considered meaningful in some figurative sense and ultimately any string of words can be made meaningful by placing it in an appropriate context but, it is believed, only certain strings have a literal meaning without the support of context. This is what we shall be studying in this chapter and it is generally taken to be the subject of semantics.

This description of semantics has been formalized in terms of the **principle of compositionality**. This states that the meaning of any construct in a language is a function of the meanings of its component parts. That is to say, morphemes are the smallest unit which can have meaning (they are the semantic atoms of the language) and the meaning of words is a function of the meaning of their morphemes. The meaning of phrases is then a function of the meaning of their words, and the meaning of sentences is a function of the meaning of their phrases. Within this view, the meaning of any complete sentence will be the same wherever and whenever it appears.

Semantics, by this definition, is concerned with the literal meaning of morphemes, words, phrases and sentences and the way that they combine. This means that such things as the meaning of utterances or dialogues (both concerned with the use of language in context) and non-literal meaning are excluded from semantics. The next chapter, which is on pragmatics, will deal with some of these wider considerations.

5.2 Semantic markers

One objective of semantic analysis is to remove from consideration sentences that are grammatical but are meaningless. For example, the grammar in Fig 3.3 will allow sentences such as

> * *The green sound holidays the stop.*

This is syntactically valid but, most people would say, quite without meaning. If we could formalize our ability to recognize meaningless constructions then we would be able to further constrain the productions of our grammar to the set of sensible sentences. Before we do so we will note that this project is not without its difficulties, for it is far more difficult to say what is meaningless than to say what is ungrammatical. We are concerned only to rule out sentences or phrases that cannot possibly have any meaning, not ones that are merely unlikely. A phrase such as *the green aunt* is meaningful even though we cannot envisage ever using it or expect to find an object that it refers to. A phrase such as *the green sound*, on the other hand, is meaningless because it fails to work as a description. There is something about the combination of these words, taken literally, that prevents it from being a referring expression at all.

If we try to say why the above sentence is meaningless, then our reasoning will probably go something like this.

(a) Only physical things can have a colour; as *sound* is not a physical object and *green* is a colour, the phrase *green sound* is meaningless.

(b) Only people can holiday. As *the sound* is not a person it cannot *holiday*.

(c) The verb *to holiday* cannot be followed by an object (NP), only a relation (expressed by a PP). That is one can *holiday in Devon*, but not * *holiday Devon*.

We can formalize the reasoning in (a) by associating with adjectives and nouns a number of semantic properties, often called **semantic markers**, which indicate the semantic categories with which the word is associated. In the sample implementation that follows we shall use the predicate *modifies* to indicate the type of object that can be modified by an adjective and the predicate *isa* to indicate the type of object that is referred to by a noun. For some sample words we might have

```
isa(aunt, human).
isa(ball,phys).
isa(bus, phys).
isa(meeting,event).
isa(sound, experience).

modifies(green, phys).
modifies(big, phys).
modifies(big, event).
```

That is, an *aunt* is human, a *ball* and a *bus* are both physical objects, a *meeting* is an event and *sound* is an experience. The adjectives *green* and *big* modify physical objects and *big* also modifies events.

Having done this we can generalize reason (a), which requires a restriction on *green* to allow it to be used only for the description of physical objects, by devising a rule for simple **nps**.

```
np --> det, adjs(A), noun(N), { n_compatible(A,N) }.
```

Prolog grammar rules allow us to add any references to normal Prolog clauses by enclosing them in curly brackets at the end of the clause. They are executed after the goals to their left have been achieved. *n_compatible* is defined as follows,

```
n_compatible([ ], _).
n_compatible([A | L], N) :-
          modifies(A, X), isa(N, X), n_compatible(L, N).
```

That is to say, a list of adjectives is *n_compatible* with a noun (N) if each adjective in the list is *n_compatible* with N. An adjective (A) is *n_compatible* with a noun (N) if it modifies objects of type X and N is an X. These rules will allow the **nps**

the green bus
the big green ball

but not

*   * the green sound*

It will also disallow the valid phrase *the green aunt,* but more about this later.

Reason (b) states that only humans can holiday, or more generally that the subject of some verbs is restricted to certain types of object. If we want to check the compatibility of a verb and its subject, then we will need to assign a semantic type to a whole phrase. The semantic category of an **np** is derived from its main noun and that of a **vp** from its main verb. So, keeping our grammar very simple, we have

np(N) --> det, adjs(A), noun(N), { n_compatible(A, N) }.

vp(V) --> verb(V).

To implement the restriction we introduce the predicate *vrule* to express the relationship between a noun and the type of thing that can be its subject. For example, we can encode the fact that only humans can holiday by

vrule(holidays, human).

We then amend Rule 1 to include a compatibility check:

s --> np(N), vp(V), { v_compatible(V, N, subj) }.

The predicate *v_compatible* is defined as

v_compatible(V, N, subj) :- vrule(V, S), isa(N, S).

According to these definitions, a subject noun (N) is compatible with a verb (V) if there is a *vrule* that allows objects of type X as the subject of V, and N is an X. This will allow sentences such as

The aunt holidays.

but not

*   * The sound holidays.*
*   * The ball holidays.*

because neither *sound* nor *ball* are human.

Reason (c) states that the verb *to holiday* cannot be followed by a noun phrase. Such restrictions may be dealt with as a matter of syntax by splitting the verb category into two new categories, transitive and intransitive verbs (see Chapter 3). Each verb would then have to be classified as one or both of these new types. In a very simple grammar the rules to handle these two categories could be represented as

    vp --> verb_trans, np.
    vp --> verb_intrans.

The dictionary can then classify *to holiday* as a *verb_intrans* and the problem is solved.

However, the proliferation of new syntactic categories leads to complexity which can be avoided by the use of semantic markers. We extend our *vrule* notation to allow a third argument corresponding to the object relation.

    vrule(holidays, human, nil).
    vrule(cancels, human, event).

These definitions mean that *to holiday* takes a human subject and no object (i.e. *nil*), whereas *to cancel* requires a human subject and an event as an object.

We then amend our code to read

    vp -->   verb(V), np(O), { v_compatible(V, O, obj) }.
    vp -->   verb(V), { v_compatible(V, nil, obj) }.

    v_compatible(V, N, subj) :-   vrule(V, S, _), isa(N, S).
    v_compatible(V, N, obj) :-   vrule(V, _, O), isa(N, O).

These rules state that a verb phrase can be a verb followed by a noun provided that the noun is compatible with the object position of the verb. Alternatively, a verb phrase can be a verb on its own provided that the object position of the verb has been explicitly disallowed. This will allow both

The aunt holidays.
The aunt cancels the meeting.

but not

* *The aunt holidays the meeting.*
* *The aunt cancels.*

One area where a system of semantic markers and restriction rules has been used effectively is in coping with lexical ambiguity in machine translation

(Wilks, 1973). Wilks developed a system known as Preference Semantics which assigned structures of semantic markers to words in the dictionary. Whenever lexical ambiguity was discovered in the input the system considered each sense of a word in turn and quantified the degree of match between the word sense and the rest of the sentence in which it appeared. Whichever sense best fitted its context would be chosen. As the context was never more than the sentence within which the ambiguous word was embedded, the principle of compositionality was not broken.

5.3 Type hierarchies

So far we have implemented, albeit in a simple form, the three reasons we gave in the previous section for rejecting the string

* *The green sound holidays the stop.*

As we try to rule out more meaningless constructs we will add more classes and will soon discover the need for discipline. Already our restrictions are a little too severe because our grammar will decide that the phrase *the green aunt* is meaningless, which it is not. This is because we assigned the word *aunt* the semantic category *human* but not that of *phys*. A simple solution to this is to simply add *phys* to the definition of *aunt*,

isa(aunt, phys).

This will work but can become very cumbersome. As we know that all humans are physical objects, we can simply record that as a single fact and amend our testing procedure accordingly. We can represent the facts by using the predicate *isa*:

isa(human, animal).
isa(animal, phys).

We then redefine *n_compatible* and *v_compatible* as follows:

n_compatible([ ], _).
n_compatible([A | L], N) :-
        modifies(A, X), really_is(N, X), n_compatible(L, N).

v_compatible(V, N, C) :- vrule(V, C = X), really_is(N, X).

The new predicate *really_is* replaces the predicate *isa* and is defined as

really_is(X, Y) :- isa(X, Y), !.
really_is(X, Y) :- isa(X, Z), really_is(Z, Y).

Hence an *aunt* is a *phys* if the following two facts are known

isa(aunt, human).
isa(human, phys).

By introducing the predicate *really_is* we are effectively developing a **type hierarchy**. That is a hierarchy of semantic categories such that each object adopts its own semantic properties and the properties of all the types in which it is included. We have done so only for nouns, but we could create a type hierarchy for adjectives and verbs also.

Exercise 5.1

Using the definitions of **s**, **np** and **vp** in Section 5.2, develop a system of semantic markers to allow the following sentences,

His voice carries.
His dog carries a stick.
His aunt hears a bang.

but not,

  * *His voice carries a stick.*
  * *His dog carries a bang.*
  * *His aunt carries.*
  * *The voice hears a bang.*

For example, we have defined the colour *green* by saying,

modifies(green, phys).

and we could continue to add such statements for all the colours. Alternatively we could define a single statement,

modifies(colour, phys).

and include statements of the form,

isa(green, colour).
isa(red, colour).

The main advantage of this would be if we wanted to allow *colour* to modify some other class of objects. Rather than writing a complete set of *modifies* clauses, one for each colour, we can add the single clause

modifies(colour,light).

We would also need to redefine *n_compatible* as

n_compatible([ ], _) :- !.
n_compatible([A I L], N) :-
        has_mod(A, X), really_is(N, X), n_compatible(L, N).

has_mod(A, X) :- modifies(A, X).
has_mod(A, X) :- isa(A, B), has_mod(B, X).

The case of verbs is particularly interesting. To apply the same principle to verbs we have to define types of verbs. For example, we might define one type as *speak_verb* which will include verbs such as *talk, say, shout, yell, phone* and *sing*. We can introduce a *v_rule* for this verb type, define instances of the verb and revise our rule for *v_compatible* accordingly.

vrule(speak_verb, subj = human).

isa(rings, speak_verb).
isa(runs, go_verb).
isa(says, speak_verb).

v_compatible(V, N, C) :- has_vrule(V, C = X), isa(N, X).

has_vrule(V, X) :- vrule(V, X).
has_vrule(V, X) :- isa(V, W), has_vrule(W, X).

Such a system may appear to have great utility, but there are dangers in applying it too simplistically. Consider a variation of the first sentence:

   * *The sound woke to the birds of John.*

This seems distinctly odd and we may wish to disallow it by insisting that only animals can *wake*. We now have the mechanism to do this by insisting that verbs like *wake* must have *subj* = *animal* as a semantic category. This will rule out the above sentence, but is it correct? We can also use the subject position to describe things that might cause John to wake, as in

The singing of birds woke John.
His aunt woke John.
The sound woke John.

If there is something semantically wrong with the original sentence it is not
that a sound cannot be the subject of *wake*, but rather that if the subject is not
animate then we expect an object that is animate. We will return to this point
in Section 5.6.

Exercise 5.2

Develop a type hierarchy for the words in the story. Show their
relationships to each other and discuss any problematic cases.

5.4 Semantic nets

Semantic nets are a general representational technique and they have been
used in natural language processing for several different purposes. One use has
been the representation of type hierarchies (see Section 5.3) and another has
been the representation of the meaning of individual sentences.

A semantic net is a **graph**, which is to say that it consists of **nodes** and **arcs**
that link nodes. The arcs are usually labelled and have a specific direction. A
common use of an arc is to represent an attribute of an entity and in this case the
arc links the entity with some value for that attribute, as in Fig 5.1.

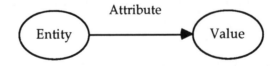

Fig 5.1 Schematic representation of an attribute arc

For example, we can use such a notation to represent the fact that all aunts are
female by Fig 5.2.

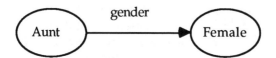

Fig 5.2 Type aunt has the gender attribute female

Here the node labelled *Aunt* is representing the type *aunt* and not any specific aunt.   Similarly, we can represent *isa* relationships between two types by means of an arc with an appropriate label. The fact that all aunts are human is represented in Fig 5.3.

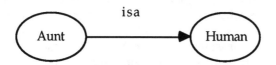

Fig 5.3 Type aunt is a subtype of type human

Figs 5.2 and 5.3 can be joined as they share the node *Aunt*. If we do this and add the fact that *Humans* have the attribute *number-of-legs* = 2, we arrive at the network in Fig 5.4.

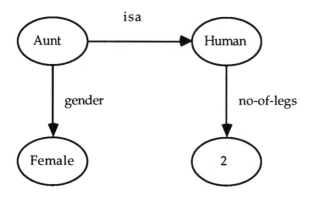

Fig 5.4   A small type hierarchy

In the previous section we implemented the inheritance of properties in terms
of Prolog code. Within semantic network notation we have to define
corresponding operations on the network. For example, an entity has not only
the attributes associated with it, but also the attributes associated with an
entity to which it is joined by an *isa* link. Using such a rule we can infer the
fact *aunts have two legs*.

To be sure that these network operations terminate and produce correct results
we have to introduce some restrictions. Firstly, there must be no cycles (i.e. we
must not be able to introduce another arc, or series of arcs, saying that *Human* is
a subtype of *Aunt*). Secondly, we must ensure that, while any type can inherit
attributes from any supertype, there must only be one value for any attribute
for any type. One way to ensure this is to make it a requirement of the
representation; the other is to make it a requirement of the implementation
that only one value is retrieved and it is always the same value.

So far our notation for semantic nets does little more than provide an
alternative representation for the type hierarchies in Section 5.3. Another use
of semantic nets is to represent the meaning of sentences, in which case the
network will have to represent specific objects as well as types. To do this we
need to introduce a notation to identify individuals from types. There are
various stylistic techniques for indicating that an entity represents a token; we
will use a colon as a prefix. So *:aunt* refers to a particular aunt and *Aunt* refers
to the type. Fig 5.5 represents the meaning of the phrase, *Aunt Jane has brown
hair*.

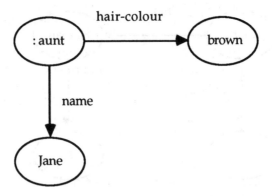

Fig 5.5 Semantic network representing the meaning of a phrase

What is of interest about semantic nets is not their representational power but the extent to which they can be used to support semantically based processing such as inference and question-answering. A sophisticated development of semantic networks to cater for difficult cases and to support a great deal of common inferencing is given by Sowa (1984).

5.5 Semantic grammar

The system of semantic markers proposed in Section 5.3 allows semantic constraints to be placed on top of pre-exisiting syntactic distinctions. The potential weakness of this approach is that the syntactic division of sentences into phrases may not correspond to the semantic divisions we require. Consider the three sentences

The 3.10 departure from Euston arrives at Birmingham at 4.50.

A train runs from Euston to Birmingham leaving at 3.10 and arriving at 4.50.

The 4.50 at Birmingham is the 3.10 from Euston.

The three sentences have different syntactic structures, but they all refer to the same underlying semantic object. If we begin with a syntactic analysis then we are committed to an intermediate structure (a parse tree) which stresses their differences and we are left with a lot of work to do if we are to achieve a common semantic representation for each of the sentences.

Suppose we abandoned syntactic categories in our grammar and used semantic categories instead? In making this change we are no longer interested whether a group of words is a noun phrase or a verb phrase, but whether it describes a station, a time, a journey etc. If the purpose of the system were restricted to accessing a database containing information about the times and status of trains, then such a grammar might be a very direct way of determining the significance of a sentence. We could start by defining four different types of sentence, one for a train's departure, one for its arrival, one for its journey and one for its status, as in Fig 5.6.

Such a grammar not only tests the grammaticality of a sentence but it produces an analysis that relates directly to the purpose of the system. For example, we know immediately that,

The Southerner gets to Taihape at 05.35.

```
S ::=    TRAIN   DEPART-VERB   STATION   TIME-PHRASE
S ::=    TRAIN   ARRIVE-VERB   STATION   TIME-PHRASE
S ::=    TRAIN   TRAVELS-VERB  from STATION to STATION
S ::=    TRAIN is STATUS
```

TRAIN ::=	the 24HR-TIME |
	TRAIN-NAME
DEPART-VERB ::=	departs | goes from | leaves [from]
ARRIVE-VERB ::=	arrives at | gets to | reaches
TRAVEL-VERB ::=	goes | runs
TIME-PHRASE ::=	at 24HR-TIME
STATUS ::=	cancelled | delayed | full | late | on time
STATION ::=	Auckland | Hamilton | Taihape | Wellington
24HR-TIME ::=	HOURS . MINUTES
TRAIN-NAME ::=	Northerner | Southerner | Silver Fern
HOURS ::=	0 .. 24
MINUTES :=	0 .. 59

Fig 5.6 A semantic grammar for a train journey database.

is a sentence about an arrival, whereas

The 12.50 is cancelled.

is a sentence about status.

Semantic grammars are particularly useful for restricted domains, but they are more difficult to control when the domain becomes larger and more general. Take our story as an example.

We can see that a lot of sentences in the story involve people going places (sentences 2, 3, 5, 6, 8, 9 and 10) and they use various verbs to achieve this (*go, leave, run, visit, board*). A first step would be to consider an abstract or generalized form of *GO* as, *someone GOES somewhere*. We can code this as in Fig 5.7.

This semantic grammar would allow sentences such as

(S5):	*He left immediately.*
(S6):	*He ran to the bus stop.*
(S8):	*It left without delay.*
(S9):	*His aunt left her house.*
(S10):	*She went on holiday.*

```
S ::=                 PERSON  GO-VERB-PH  [ DESTINATION ]

PERSON ::=            PERSON-NAME  |
                      PERSON-PRONOUN  |
                      DET  PERSON-NOUN

GO-VERB-PH ::=        GO-VERB  [ ADVERB-PH ]  [ PREP ]
ADVERB-PH ::=         ADVERB  |
                      PREP  TIME-PH

DESTINATION ::=       PLACE-NAME  |
                      [ DET ]  PLACE-NOUN

DET ::=                    a | an | her | his | the
PERSON-NAME ::=            John
PERSON-PRONOUN ::=        he | she | they
PERSON-NOUN ::=           aunt | man | uncle | woman

GO-VERB ::=               left | went | ran
PREP ::=                  for | on | to | without
ADVERB ::=                immediately | quickly
TIME-PH ::=               delay | hours

PLACE-NAME ::=            Devon
PLACE NOUN ::=            bus stop | holiday | station
```

Fig 5.7 A semantic grammar for people going places

It would not, however, allow sentences such as

    * *The bus stop left its house.*

as the phrase *the bus stop* describes a destination not a person.

If we were to try to provide a semantic grammar for the whole of our story we would need to add definitions describing acts of communication and mental acts. We would also need to have some objective in doing so, perhaps the creation of a database containing the facts of the story which could be queried later.

Exercise 5.3

Devise a semantic grammar to describe speak-acts such as *rang* and *told* as used in

> *He rang the station to discover the times of trains.*
> *A clerk told him that all of the trains were running but one of them was already full.*
> *He told his mother that he was going.*

5.6 Semantic cases

In Section 5.2 we used the distinction between verbs that take an object and those that do not. At the surface level the matter is more complicated because certain verbs can take two objects, for example,

> *John gave his aunt a letter.*

Suppose we were to allow for this in our definition of a sentence:

S ::= NP VP [NP] [NP] PP*

We can identify the role, or **case**, of each of the NPs by calling the one before the **VP** the **subject**, and those following the **VP** the **indirect object** and the **direct object**, respectively. We shall later include PPs in our analysis where each **PP** describes an object in its NP and adopts a case from its preposition. These are the **surface cases** which describe the surface structure of sentences, as in Fig 5.8.

> John woke.
> **subject** = John
>
> John woke his aunt.
> **subject** = John ; **dir-obj** = his aunt
>
> John gave his aunt a letter.
> **subject** = John ; **ind-obj** = his aunt ; **dir-obj** = a letter

Fig 5.8 Surface cases

Next we need to classify verbs into those that take neither type of object (e.g. *to holiday*), those that do not take an indirect object (e.g. *to wake*) and those that take both types of object (e.g. *to give*). With proper controls we can then say

John holidays.
John wakes his aunt.
John gave his aunt a letter.

but not

* *John holidays his aunt.*
* *John woke his aunt a letter.*

Whilst this is an important first step, the analysis of surface cases is not adequate to explain all of the restrictions on meaningful sentences, or to explain how a common meaning is attributable to different surface forms. Consider the first two examples in Fig 5.8,

John woke.
John woke his aunt.

Whilst *John* is the subject of both of these sentences, it is John who wakes up in the first and his aunt who wakes up in the second. In the second sentence John is the person who caused the event. If we wish to explain that *John* in the first sentence fulfills the same semantic role as *his aunt* in the second, then we have to develop a notion of semantic, or **deep cases** (see also Section 3.7). In this terminology the person who brings the event about is the **agent** and the person who is affected by the event is the **theme**. The same three sentences and their semantic cases are shown in Fig 5.9.

John woke.
theme = John

John woke his aunt.
agent = John ; **theme** = his aunt

John gave his aunt a letter.
agent = John ; **recipient-to** = his aunt ; **theme** = a letter

Fig 5.9 Semantic cases

There are restrictions on the semantic cases that a verb may adopt, just as there are restrictions on its surface cases. For example, the verb *to wake* must always take a theme and it may take an agent.

In order to derive deep cases from surface cases we require a set of rules. These should be independent of particular verbs, for example,

If the direct object is present
then (subject = agent & direct object = theme)
else   (subject = theme)

We can encode this in Prolog as follows. First we define the limitations on surface cases.

scase(wake, [subj = yes, dobj = maybe]).

This says that the verb *to wake* must have a subject and may have a direct object. The omission of a case means that it is forbidden so there is no need for a clause [... , iobj = no]. Next we define the limitations on deep cases.

dcase(wake, [theme = yes, agent = maybe]).

This says that the verb *to wake* must have a theme and may have an agent. We then define our grammar rule for sentences as

s(Deep_Cases) -->
        np(Subj), vp(Verb), poss_np(IObj), poss_np(DObj),
        { convert(Subj, Verb, IObj, DObj, Deep_Cases) }.

This allows the clause *convert* to do all the work in transforming surface to deep cases and checking that cases are valid. The main definition of *convert* is given in Fig 5.10 and the full program is given in Appendix 3.

```
convert(Subj, Verb, IObj, DObj, Deep_Cases) :-
    scase_agreement(Verb, Subj, IObj, Dobj) ,
    scase_to_dcase(Subj, IObj, DObj, Deep_Cases),
    dcase_agreement(Verb, Deep_cases).

scase_agreement(Verb, Subj, IObj, Dobj) :-
    scase(Verb,S_Cases)
    agreement(S_Cases, [subj = Subj, iobj = IObj, dobj = DObj])

scase_to_dcase(Subj, _, nil, [theme = Subj]) :- !.
scase_to_dcase(Subj, _, DObj, [agent = Subj, theme = DObj]).

dcase_agreement(Verb, Deep_cases) :-
    dcase(Verb,D_Cases),
    agreement(D_Cases, Deep_Cases).
```

%   agreement checks that all present cases are permitted and all necessary cases are present

Fig 5.10 Outline Prolog code for a simple case grammar

This example may explain the principle of case grammar but is not sufficient to begin to explain the sophistication of natural language and it should not surprise you to know that many different systems of deep cases have been proposed. Fig 5.11 shows a very basic set of cases that will serve to explain some interesting features of some verbs in our story.

Case	Description
AGENT	The person who caused the event to happen
THEME	The thing affected by the event
INSTRUMENT	The tool used in causing the event
SOURCE	The origin in some state change
GOAL	The destination in some state change
LOCATION	The place where the event occurred

Fig 5.11 A set of common cases

Using these cases, we can describe two of the verbs in our story as follows.

scase(send, [subj = yes, iobj = maybe, dobj = maybe]).
scase(cancel, [subj = yes, dobj = maybe]).

dcase(send, [agent = maybe, theme = yes, instrument = maybe, source = maybe, goal = maybe]).
dcase(cancel, [agent = maybe, theme = yes, instrument = maybe, location = maybe]).

We will also define two types of sentence, those in the active and those in the passive mood.

```
s(Deep_Cases) -->
        np(Subj), vp(Verb), poss_np(IObj), poss-np(DObj), pps(Ps),
        { convert(active, Subj, Verb, IObj, DObj, Ps, Deep_Cases) }.

s(Deep_Cases) -->
        np(Subj), [was], vp(Verb), pps(Ps),
        { convert(passive, Subj, Verb, nil, nil, Ps, Deep_Cases) }.
```

Note that passive sentences are not allowed to take any objects.   For illustration we can define the following *nps* and *vps,*

> np(john) --> ['John'].
> np(train) --> [train].
> np(house) --> [home].
> np(london) --> ['London'].
> np(devon) --> ['Devon'].
> np(letter) --> [letter].
> np(meeting) --> [the, meeting].
> np(luggage) --> [his, luggage].
>
> vp(send) --> [sent].
> vp(cancel) --> [cancelled].

The rules for conversion from surface to deep cases are given in Fig 5.12

For active sentences:

> The subject is the agent, else it is the instrument.
> If not the subject, the instrument is indicated by *by* or *with.*
> The direct object is the theme.
> The source is indicated by *from.*
> The goal is indicated by the indirect object, else by *to.*
> The location can only be present if there is an agent.
> The location is indicated by *from.*

For passive sentences:

> The subject is the theme.
> The agent is indicated by *by.*
> The instrument is indicated by *by* or *with.*
> The source is indicated by *from.*
> The goal is indicated by *to.*
> The location can only be present if there is an agent.
> The location is indicated by *from.*

Fig 5.12   Rules for converting surface to deep cases

The first example will be recognized as an active sentence and result in the following deep cases.

> *John sent his luggage from London to Devon by train.*
> **agent** = john, **theme** = luggage, **instrument** = train,
> **source** = london, **goal** = devon

The same deep case assignments could also generate sentences such as

> *The train sent his luggage from London to Devon.*
> *His luggage was sent by John from London to Devon by train.*

but not, for example,

> * *His luggage sent the train from London to Devon.*

The second example will be recognized as a passive sentence and result in the following deep cases.

> *The meeting was cancelled by John by letter from home.*
> **agent** = john ; **theme** = meeting ; **instrument** = letter ;
> **location** = house

The same deep cases can generate the following sentences.

> *John cancelled the meeting by letter from home.*
> *The letter cancelled the meeting.*
> *The meeting was cancelled.*

Exercise 5.4

Using the notation develop in Section 5.6, define the verb *to tell* so that the sentence

> *John told the man that he was resigning by letter from home.*

will be recognized as an active sentence and result in the following deep cases.

> **agent** = john ; **theme** = resigning ; **instrument** = letter ;
> **goal** = man ; **location** = house

What other sentences could these deep cases generate?

As a grammar, the system of cases we have described is still overproductive in that it is capable of generating many meaningless sentences. It can be improved by assigning types to noun phrases as we did in Section 5.3, and by restricting the type of noun that can occupy the various case slots. For example, we might vary *dcase* as follows,

```
dcase( cancel, [ agent = maybe/human,
                 theme = yes/event,
                 instrument = maybe/media,
                 location = maybe/place]).
```

meaning that the agent of *to cancel* must be human, the theme must be an event, etc. We can then introduce *isa* relations,

```
isa(man, human).
isa(john, man).
isa(meeting, event).
isa(letter, media).
isa(phone, media).
isa(house, place).
isa(london, place).
```

This will allow us productions such as,
John cancels the meeting.
The meeting was cancelled by phone.

but not

* *The meeting cancels John.*
* *The phone was cancelled by the meeting.*

By adding type checking to our case grammar system we can eliminate many meaningless statements from our productions.

The ELI system mentioned in Chapter 4 used a version of case grammar to express semantic relations. For its deep cases it used a notation known as **conceptual dependency** (CD). CD uses the cases ACTOR, OBJECT, DIR-TO, DIR-FROM, RECIP-TO, RECIP-FROM and INSTRUMENT and is also able to represent possessives, states, attributes and a number of more complex aspects of natural language. A particular feature of CD is that INSTRUMENT case in not an object but another CD representation (i.e. an event).

Traditionally CD representations are diagrams that provide a mental picture of the meaning of a sentence and can be quite appealing. Their transformation into a list structure reduces this appeal but, of course, provides a form in which processing can be achieved. Fig 5.13 shows the CD-diagram and list structure for the sentence, *John ran to the bus stop.*

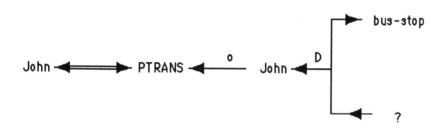

$$\text{PTRANS} \, (\, \text{ACTOR} = \text{John}, \; \text{OBJECT} = \text{John}, \; \text{DIR-TO} = \text{bus\_stop} \,)$$

Fig 5.13 Conceptual dependency representations

Section 4.5 shows how an expectation-based parser can be used to derive such a representation from natural language text in simple cases.

Case grammars enjoyed some popularity during the 1970s (see Fillmore, 1968; Bruce, 1975). Though they are not widely used today the idea of cases is important as a case grammar system with type checking can reduce the number of meaningless statements and provide a direct means of achieving a semantic representation. However, it is very difficult to devise an adequate general set of cases and to specify the rules that translate from surface structure to deep cases in unrestricted natural language.

5.7 Logical semantics

One idea about meaning is that the meaning of a word like *train* is somehow linked to the set of things that we call a train.   Not all the words in our language are as easy to explain as nouns, though we might think that case grammar gives us an idea of how to describe the meaning of prepositions, for example.   A particularly difficult category of word to describe is the quantifier, which includes words such as *all, some* and *none.* Such words do not seem to refer to any specific object or property but they do have a precise function when we come to making inferences.

First we must select an MRL that will explain quantification and inference. First order predicate calculus (FOPC) has been designed with just that in mind, so seems an obvious choice. If you are unfamiliar with the notation of FOPC consult a logic textbook such as Mendelson (1987). The major purpose of the notation is to allow proper inferences to take place and we will accept that FOPC has a well defined meaning in this regard. The task remains of translating English sentences that contain quantifiers into statements in FOPC.

FOPC uses two quantifiers which indicate the nature and scope of variables. The universal quantifier (formally written as $\forall$) is informally interpreted as being *for all*. The existential quantifier (formally written as $\exists$) is informally interpreted as being *there exists*. As the formal symbols are not present on most keyboards we shall, in our programming, use the symbols *forall* to represent universal quantification and *exists* to represent existential quantification.

The task before us, then, is to translate natural language sentences such as

All of the trains are running.
One of the trains is full.

into the FOPC formulae

forall(X) : (train(X) -> running(X))
exists(Y) : (train(Y) & full(Y))

which can be interpreted less formally as

For all objects X, if X is a train then X is running.
There exists an object, Y, that is a train and it is full.

We can realize these formulae quite simply using Prolog grammar rules. First we need to define some special symbols.

:- op(30, xfy, '=>').
:- op(28, xfy, ':').
:- op(26, xfy, '&').

We can now use these freely as infix operators to define structures. The basic principles are given in Periera & Warren (1980), which we shall adapt for our purposes.

Whilst this may cater for straightforward examples, determining the correct FOPC formula for every sentence in natural language is not easy. The determiner *a* (or *an*), for example, is often taken to refer to one individual (i.e. to indicate the existential quantifier), as in

A bird is flying.
exists(X) : (bird(X) & flying(X))

However, it can also be used to refer to one species, indicating the universal quantifier, as in

A bird is an animal.
forall(X) : (bird(X) => animal(X))

s(P) --> np(X, VP, P), vp(X, VP).

np(X, VP, P) --> quant(X, NNP, VP, P), [of, the], noun(X, NNP).

vp(X, P) --> be, adj(X, P).

quant(X, NNP, VP, forall(X) : (NNP => VP)) --> [all].
quant(X, NNP, VP, exists(X) : (NNP & VP)) --> [one].

noun(X, train(X)) --> [trains].

be--> [are].
be --> [is].

adj(X, full(X)) --> [full].
adj(X, running(X)) --> [running].

Fig 5.14 Handling quantification in DCGs

Exercise 5.5

Determine the correct FOPC formula for the compound sentence

None of the trains are cancelled but one of the trains is full.

Amend the coding in Fig 5.14 to cater for the words *none, cancelled* and *but.*

Whilst there are many other problems in trying to translate from natural language to FOPC, there are also many shortcomings with FOPC as an MRL for the purpose of inference. For example, the use of modals such as *can, may* and *must,* and of adverbs such as *necessarily* and *possibly,* cannot be fully represented in FOPC in a manner that allows regular inferencing. To handle such terms requires a **modal logic.**

If we wish to reason about time then we will need to be able to record the salient features of each tense and aspect, such as whether the event happened in the past, present or future, whether it was an instantaneous event or a continuous process, and if it was the latter whether it has started and/or been completed. To encode such information we require a **tense logic**.

There are also problems representing Sentence 4 in our story, which, in its entirety, says

S4:   *A clerk told him that none of the trains were cancelled but one of them was already full.*

We have indicated a FOPC representation for the meaning of the phrase *None of the trains are cancelled but one of them is full* but not of the whole sentence. It may seem that this is no serious problem as we can find a FOPC formula that can combine the meaning of this phrase with that of,*A clerk told him that ...* to produce the meaning of the whole sentence. For example, *A clerk told John that all of the trains were running* might erroneously be represented in FOPC as

exists(C) : (clerk(C) & exists(J) : (John(J) & forall(T) : (train(T) =>
running(T) & told(C, J, T))))

The problem with doing this is that FOPC formulae are first and foremost concerned with the preservation of truth, and the truth of the phrase *All of the trains are running ...* has nothing to do with the truth of the sentence as a whole. In fact all combinations of truth values are possible: if the clerk has been telling the truth then both the phrase and the sentence are true; if the clerk has been deliberately lying then the phrase is false but the sentence true; if the clerk has not said anything of the kind then the sentence is false regardless of whether the phrase is true or false.

What we want to say is that, in the context of this sentence, the phrase *All of the trains are running ...* has a different kind of meaning from the sentence as a whole. We say that the sentence as a whole has an **extensional** meaning, whilst the phrase within it has an **intensional** meaning.

We can explain the difference between extensional and intensional meanings by considering a noun phrase like *John's oldest living aunt*. The extensional meaning is identified with the thing or set of things that the phrase refers to in the real world. In this case the phrase may identify a certain individual, who may also be known by the name *Aunt Jane*. These two phrases therefore refer to the same object, which we must distinguish from all of the phrases used to identify her, so we will call her *Aunt-Jane'*. We can therefore say that

Aunt-Jane' is the extensional meaning or **reference** of the phrase *John's oldest living aunt.*

The intensional meaning is not concerned with the thing referred to by a phrase but is an expression of its sense. The intensional meaning of the above phrase might be,

> *the sister of the mother or father of John who is alive and who is older than any other sister of the mother or father of John.*

It is argued that one reason why we need intensional objects is that when, for example, Aunt Jane dies, *Aunt-Molly'* may become the reference of the phrase *John's oldest living aunt,*but we would not want to say that the meaning of the phrase has thereby changed. We can now say that the extension of the phrase will change on the death of *Aunt-Jane'* but the intension will remain the same.

Returning now to our Sentence 4, we need to apply this distinction to phrases and sentences. The extensional meaning of any sentence can be equated to its truth or falsity in the real world. Either the situation it describes is true or it is false. The intensional meaning is a form of mental object and does not have the implication that it is true in the world. We can therefore say that the phrase *All of the trains are running ...* has an intensional meaning in this sentence whereas the phrase *A clerk told him ...* has an extensional meaning.

What we therefore require is an MRL that will allow us to represent something like

> **extension** { A clerk told him that
>   **intension** { all of the trains are running } }

Most of these limitations of FOPC have been overcome in a formal language called IL and developed by Montague (1974), who has had a great influence on formal semantics. IL is a very comprehensive MRL but both the procedures for translating from natural language to IL and those for carrying out inference in IL are extremely complex.

So far we have considered semantics purely in terms of conversion into a MRL that will serve some particular purpose we have. For some people, notably linguists and philosophers, this is not enough and the real semantics of natural language must involve reference to the real world (Lewis, 1972). Ideally we would want to specify referential links between symbols of an MRL and objects and properties of the real world.

Philosophers have investigated such links and have found problems with simplistic approaches. The practice among logicians is to consider an abstract model of the real world (for example, the set of all possible worlds) as being the basis of a referential definition of an MRL. This has proved particularly useful for modal, tense and similar logics.

5.8 Summary

Semantic processing has several purposes. It can be used to restrict an overproductive context free grammar so that only meaningful sentences are produced. To do so one may use semantic markers and a type hierarchy. It can also be used to derive some representation of the meaning of a sentence so that further processing can take place. This may require the development of a semantic grammar, a case grammar or some logical formalism.

Throughout this Chapter we have limited our horizons by adopting the view that we are concerned only with the literal meaning of a sentence. By this we not only mean that we are ignoring any figurative use of language but we are also ignoring the fact that the meaning of a sentence alters when it is used in different situations. Our approach may have reduced the problem to a manageable size but it is not credible as a long-term solution. Even for such an obvious reason as pronoun reference (how do we know that *He* in sentence 2 refers to *John* in sentence 1?) we need to analyse the interaction of sentences in the story. The limitations of the view adopted in this Chapter and systems that transcend these limitations will be discussed under the heading of Pragmatics in the next Chapter.

6

Pragmatics

6.1 Reference and anaphoric links

The term **pragmatics** is used to cover a range of ways in which the broader setting of a sentence is important for determining its correct interpretation. In this chapter we shall look at some ways in which the linguistic context and knowledge of the world needs to be taken account of in order to understand a sentence as produced on some particular occasion. We shall look at the way a dialogue has a structure which can be relevant to the interpretation of a sentence and the way the purpose of a remark can be different from its apparent form.

Semantics is usually restricted to dealing with the meanings of sentences as they are determined by the meanings of their parts. But sentences are not merely understood individually. Rather one arrives at an interpretation of a whole story, speech or conversation which is not the mere aggregation of the separate meanings of individual sentences. This is clear enough even in our simple text.

The reference of *his* in

It was the first day of his summer holidays and he was going to stay with his aunt who lived in Devon.

is to *John*, mentioned in the previous sentence,

John woke to the sound of birds.

Where the reference of a pronoun, say, is determined by it being linked with a word or phrase occurring previously we speak of an **anaphoric** link.

The noun phrase *a clerk* in

A clerk told him that none of the trains were cancelled but one of them was already full.

clearly refers to the person at the other end of the telephone in the telephone call mentioned in

Visiting aunts can be fun so he rang the station to discover the times of trains.

assuming *rang* has been correctly interpreted.

In the context of the story one understands

He decided to leave immediately

as meaning that he decided to leave for his holidays in Devon.

In the sixth sentence we are told that

He ran to the bus stop.

How does that relate to the surrounding remarks about leaving and being at the train station?

We shall look at a variety of approaches for dealing with these issues.

We have seen in Chapter 5 how, in the tradition of logical semantics, the meaning of an MRL (meaning representation language) is given in terms of reference. In order to deal with the initial occurrence of a proper name like *John* in a text it suffices to establish a unique name in the MRL, perhaps *JOHN1*. Similarly, to handle the first occurrence of *John's aunt*, one could establish a unique name in the MRL, and in addition establish the relation with *JOHN1*. What fixes the link between *JOHN1* and the real John in the world will not be investigated here. The problem that concerns us comes in handling coreference, where later expressions have to be identified as referring to an individual already introduced.

In principle there is no definitive reason why semantics must be restricted to the unit of the sentence. In fact anaphoric links, as between *his* and *John*, might at first seem to fall naturally within the sphere of semantics, whether they occur within a sentence or not. That would seem to follow from the assumption that semantics involves reference.

However, in practice, anaphoric links between sentences, even more than links within sentences, appear not to depend consistently on precise rules based on sentence structure.

One simple proposal to deal with *his* in the example above is to link it anaphorically with the previous male NP in the text. It would be straightforward to maintain a register of the last mentioned male NP and similarly for female NPs and neuter NPs. However that gives counterintuitive results for some texts. Suppose the preceding sentence were,

> *John was full of excitement when he spoke to his brother.*

The *his* in the following sentence might well be intended to refer back to John, but according to this proposal it would refer to his brother. Another possible proposal might determine the anaphoric link as being the subject of the previous sentence. However the start of a rather different story might be

> *Mr. Major, John's boss, told him he was very sorry to have to bother him at home.*

Surely the *his* in the second sentence would normally be taken to refer back to *John* once again rather than the subject (*Mr. Major*). Moreover, this does not appear to be an effect that depends purely on surface syntax and is unlikely to be resolved at the level of semantic representation either.

Exercise 6.1

With reference to the story, why is the *he* in the fifth sentence not anaphorically linked to *a clerk* in the fourth?

Determining coreference is only one part of the problem; we also have to identify and deal with newly mentioned items. We have already mentioned the need to establish new symbols for newly mentioned items.

There are, however, many traps in dealing with the reference of noun phrases. As we saw in Section 5.7, some phrases are not referential at all. For example, *a sea monster* need not be referential in

> *John believes there is a sea monster off the coast of Devon.*

Believes and similar mental words create what are known as **intensional contexts** in which it is possible that there is no referent.

A different kind of problem arises when a phrase could refer to a species in one context but to a member of the species in another, as in

> *The whale is an intelligent mammalian species.*
> *The whale struck the ship towards the stern.*

There are many more such problems and we are not going to be able to resolve them all. However we can look at the prospects for establishing an appropriate model for the structure of a text that can assist with some of the problems of anaphoric reference and a range of other things besides.

6.2 Pragmatics in SHRDLU

Terry Winograd's SHRDLU system (1972), although some twenty years old now, is an impressively complete natural language system. It is worth looking there first for some techniques for dealing with some of the kinds of problems we have been mentioning.

The work concerned a blocks world consisting of cubes, pyramids, boxes etc. of various colours and sizes. The world was sufficiently circumscribed so that a complete description of the state of the world could be achieved, but there is sufficient complexity in the world for definite descriptions such as *the pyramid* or *the large block* to be ambiguous in their reference.

The structure of the system does not include any explicit mention of pragmatics. But many of the procedures it employs to, say, interpret the meaning of noun phrases, while described as semantic, could reasonably be thought of as pragmatic.

To interpret *the*, the system looks either for a unique object in the blocks world of the specified kind or a unique one that has been mentioned in the previous sentence. Thus, *the pyramid*, when not following a sentence containing a phrase referring to a pyramid, will be rejected by the system as ambiguous, like this:

> *I DON'T UNDERSTAND WHICH PYRAMID YOU MEAN*

If, on the other hand, the previous sentence contained the phrase *the blue pyramid*, then the phrase *the pyramid* is understood as referring to the blue pyramid. Certain pieces of information are retained from the previous sentence, such as the time, place and objects mentioned. In fact the whole of the previous sentence can be referred to in a question like, *Why did you do that? (ibid* p.33).

Here we have an example of a simple mechanism for creating links between sentences. Winograd recognized that in principle one should not only handle the local discourse context, linking back to the previous sentence, but also the overall discourse context which depends on the general topic of the whole discussion (in this case, the blocks world). We shall return to that soon.

The system contains a description of the nature of the world, descriptions of the various blocks, and also the current situation of those blocks. An interpretation of an instruction to the system such as

Put the little red block on the big blue cube.

involves not only the realization of what state the sentence aims to achieve but also the procedures that need to be done to achieve that state, such as clearing the blocks off another block that is required to be moved.

It is a significant feature of the work that meaning is not merely expressed in an MRL but is reflected ultimately in terms of interactions with a world, albeit a world of a circumscribed nature. We can be confident of a person's grasp of a natural language because their interaction with their environment is appropriate to their utterances and those of others. Similarly, SHRDLU responds appropriately to linguistic instructions both verbally and in terms of its actions in the blocks world.

In particular it can explain why it did various things. If it needed to clear a block off the big blue cube as a precondition for placing the little red block on the big blue cube it retains a representation of that inference and can produce the explanation.

The way in which SHRDLU uses natural language in the context of its blocks world and the manipulation of blocks is relevant to pragmatics in a broad sense, as pragmatics can be understood to concern the use of language in a context. However our main concern is with resolving uncertainties of interpretation. Here is an important further aspect of the system which is relevant to that.

The SHRDLU system allows knowledge of the world to be considered while a sentence is being parsed. This means that a syntactically reasonable parse which is incompatible with the state of the world is discarded at an early stage. This increases efficiency as well as corresponding to human processing practices. The instruction

Put the blue pyramid on the block in the box.

has two possible syntactic analyses depending on whether *the blue pyramid on the block* is grouped together or *the block in the box* is. SHRDLU is able to check whether *the blue pyramid on the block* makes sense in the scene and, if not, discards the corresponding syntactic analysis.

Returning to our story, in the sentence

He boarded the Devon train with his luggage and it left without delay.

the normal interpretation would be that he took the luggage on board with him rather than boarded the train which already carried his luggage. (In syntactic terms, *with his luggage* is a PP which modifies *boarded* not part of an NP, *the Devon train with his luggage*). Achieving that interpretation depends on our general knowledge about how we normally deal with luggage in our society. This is not as easily handled as the blocks world case, but we can make some progress with a different kind of approach.

Exercise 6.2

Describe a context in which *the Devon train with his luggage* is correctly understood as a constituent NP.

6.3 Frames and scripts

When we leave the limited arena of a blocks world and consider text relating to a more realistic world, even one as mundane as that described by our story, we find there is an explosion in the level of detail and in ways of expressing ideas and a corresponding difficulty in identifying links between different parts of the text.

We as human subjects can understand how the various sentences cohere to tell a story. But there does not seem to be a straightforward account, lending itself to automation, of how the various activities involved in setting off on a trip fit together. For example, how does running to the bus stop fit in with the other events? So much seems to be left implicit.

In the blocks world, on the other hand, a procedure of moving a certain block to a certain location can be relatively easily decomposed into the component actions of clearing another block off the top of the one to be moved and so on. What we need is a framework that captures the main lines of what is going on so that ambiguities can be resolved and gaps can be filled in. Achieving that framework could seem like a very tall order indeed, requiring an understanding of the human mind at its most subtle and complex.

The task can be made more manageable if we consider separately each kind of situation or object we are talking about. Then perhaps the framework we need just reflects the background of general knowledge that anyone growing up in the relevant culture would naturally acquire about that kind of thing. This background knowledge can give us a set of expectations about a particular situation, such as going on holiday. We have already seen the value of expectation-driven processes with respect to parsing in Chapter 4.

This general idea has been developed in artificial intelligence in work on knowledge representation. The initial work was based on Minsky's notion of a frame (Minsky, 1975). A frame is intended to model the background knowledge about some topic.

Computationally a frame is a data structure containing a number of specified slots. Default values can be specified for these slots. This represents a background assumption about what usually exists or happens, an assumption which can be overridden. Usually values are determined by special procedures called demons. One way a demon can determine a value is by actively searching the text for information that settles it. Demons are often executed provided a condition is satisfied.

A script is a frame-like data structure for describing a typical sequence of events. It has slots for which values are actively sought in the same way as a frame, but the emphasis is on the temporal ordering. This reflects a person's expectations about what is likely to happen next in a situation. See Schank & Abelson (1977) for a comprehensive overview of the area. Fig 6.1 contains a schematic example of a frame and some scripts that might be relevant to our story.

HOLIDAY frame

Specialization_of: TIME_OFF

Holidayer:

    range: a PERSON_NAME

Host:

    range: a PERSON_NAME or PERSON_NP

Destination:

    range: a PLACE_NAME

Event_sequence:

    default: GOING_ON_HOLIDAY script

GOING_ON_HOLIDAY script

Roles: (Holidayer of HOLIDAY, Host of HOLIDAY)

Point_of_view: Holidayer

Event_sequence:
    first: PLAN_VISIT script
    then: OUTWARD_JOURNEY script
    then: DESTINATION_TIME script
    then: RETURN_JOURNEY script

OUTWARD_JOURNEY script

Props: (Home_bus_stop, Home_train_station,
         Destination_train_station, Destination_bus_stop, Home of host)

Roles: (Holidayer of GOING_ON_HOLIDAY, Host of
         GOING_ON_HOLIDAY)

Point_of_view: Holidayer

Event_sequence:
    first: walk or run to Home_bus_stop
    then: take bus from Home_bus_stop to Home_train_station
    then: take train from Home_train_station to
             Destination_train_station
    then: take bus from Destination_train_station to
             Destination_bus_stop
    then: walk or run from Destination_bus_stop to Home of Host

Fig 6.1 A frame and some scripts for going on holiday

This illustrates the intended structure of frames and scripts. It is not expressed in the original notation but in the near English style employed in Barr and Feigenbaum (1981). The HOLIDAY frame is indicated here as a special case of a more general frame TIME_OFF, the frame covering all kinds of time off from work or school. The idea is that the general characteristics of TIME_OFF are inherited into holiday. Perhaps TIME_OFF includes a default value for enjoyment level, namely, high. This would automatically apply to HOLIDAY as well.

We talk of a frame for a holiday, rather than a script, because a holiday is viewed as an object, albeit an abstract one, rather than a sequence of events at this level of analysis. One could also have a frame for a station or a house. The sequence of events gets covered in scripts at lower levels. Clearly the frame and scripts in the example are for illustration rather than being definitive models.

Frames and scripts can be conveniently represented in Prolog. Here are a few hints as to how the representation might go. One can express the value of a particular slot for a particular frame in this form

    Frame(Slot,Value)

    e.g.   holiday(holidayer, john)
            holiday(specialization_of, time_off)

This gives us a simple way of expressing the values of the slots once they have been extracted from the text. It is then easy to retrieve information with a predicate *value* with this form:

    value(Frame, Slot, Value)

Thus one could retrieve a value in this example like this:

    ?- value(holiday, holidayer, X).

    X = john

That is the most straightforward case. However, sometimes a value needs to be determined indirectly, for example in the case,

    ?- value(holiday, enjoyment_value, X).

For a treatment of the inheritance of values from higher level frames, which is needed here, see Bratko (1990).

The example frame and scripts let us see some prospects for bringing out meanings in our story that are not explicit. Each slot requires a demon for finding the appropriate value in the text. These procedures will operate in interaction with the work done by the parser and semantic processor. Clearly a sophisticated language processor will have to recognize a huge variety of synonymous expressions in order to cope with the varied ways that a step in a script can be expressed.

Our story would provide an instance of the HOLIDAY frame with these values:

HOLIDAY frame

Specialization_of:	TIME_OFF
Holidayer:	*John*
Host:	*John's aunt*
Destination:	*Devon*
Event_Sequence:	default: GOING_ON_HOLIDAY script

The parts of the event sequence of the GOING_ON_HOLIDAY script that are relevant to the text are the PLAN_VISIT script, and the OUTWARD_JOURNEY script. The PLAN_VISIT script is not supplied, but clearly the telephone call to the station would be relevant to it. The OUTWARD_JOURNEY script is interesting in relation to the text, as much for what is left out of the text as for what is included. Our program needs to relate running to the bus stop (in Sentence 6) to the rest of the story. This can be identified as the first step of the event sequence. What the script fills in for us by default is that this is followed by catching a bus to the railway station. The next step, taking the train to the destination train station, is briefly mentioned (in Sentence 8), in terms of the Devon train leaving.

Going back a little, how do we interpret Sentence 5,

> *He decided to leave immediately*

as meaning, in effect,

> *He decided to leave immediately for his holidays in Devon. ?*

Having *Devon* settled as the value for **Destination** in the HOLIDAY frame is part of the process. Then the program needs to identify the sentence as relating to the outward journey step in the event sequence for the GOING_ON_HOLIDAY script.

Note that *leave* does not in itself correspond to any of the steps in the event sequence for the OUTWARD_JOURNEY script. We could infer its relationship to one or more of the steps or, more likely, it would be one of the things that can cue the script, that is, bring the particular script into operation.

Exercise 6.3

How should *her house* in the ninth sentence be interpreted in the structure of the frame and scripts? What assumptions are embodied in the frame and scripts (and demons) that relate to this? What facts in a similar story might make these assumptions inappropriate?

There are two main worries about the frames and scripts approach as a realistic model of human psychology. The same worries may extend to their practical usefulness in natural language understanding by machine. The first is that one would need to know a huge number of frames and scripts in order to deal with an ordinary week's worth of conversations. The second is that one would need to quickly and accurately select the correct frame or script from among that huge selection.

An approach that is more general and thus involves less storage of highly specific objects is to use **plans**. Consider the rather artificial OUTWARD_JOURNEY script that was given above. Could the structure we find here not be inferred from knowledge that is less specific? For example, if you want to go to a certain place then you have to get there using one of various possible modes of transport.

Schank and Abelson's work on plans is designed to coexist with the work on scripts, but captures the more general level of structure. Rather than have a complete script for something like going on holiday, the structure can be built up on the basis of knowing the various means for achieving different kinds of goals. We start with a main goal and work back to some means for achieving it. That defines some subgoals which we also need to find some means of achieving. The process is repeated until we have a set of actions which are regarded as primitive, at which point we have a plan. To plan in this way we need a goal to be associated with a set of standard ways of accomplishing the goal.

Here is how the specification of standard ways of achieving goals can be used to bring out the structure found in the OUTWARD_JOURNEY script. The goal of going on holiday requires travelling to the destination. The standard way of travelling a medium length distance is by train (let us suppose). What one has to do to travel by train is to travel the fairly short distance to the local train station, take the train to the destination train station, and travel the fairly short distance from the destination train station to the precise destination. The standard way of travelling a fairly short distance is by bus, and so forth.

The notion of planning is well established in artificial intelligence. One major area of application is that of a robot planning its actions. SHRDLU creates a plan when it works out what needs to be done in order to move a block to a certain place. We can say that a precondition of moving a block is that its top is clear. That specifies a sub-goal that needs to be achieved. Achieving that sub-goal may require a further precondition to be met, and so on. In Chapter 7 we shall see how a notion of planning can also be applied to language generation.

6.4 The structure of dialogue

We have seen how understanding utterances can depend in various ways on knowing what the world is like, either in terms of characteristic patterns of events or simply knowing the details of the current situation. But pragmatics does not always represent that kind of retreat from the linguistic.

We asked at the beginning of the chapter *Why stop at sentences?* We first of all considered whether semantics should stop at sentences. What about syntax? Of course syntax could be considered to stop at sentences by definition. But just as there are well defined structures within sentences so there may be well defined structures in conversations.

Of course, a monologue and particularly a prepared speech can have a well defined structure. But what is more striking is that a dialogue, where no single participant can totally control the direction, also appears to have significant structure. Just as one's implicit knowledge of syntactic structure contributes to one's understanding of the meaning of a sentence, so one's implicit knowledge of discourse structure contributes to one's understanding of the individual sentence in the context of the whole discussion.

Each level of linguistic description requires a set of concepts with which to express the structures and regularities at that level. What are the appropriate concepts to talk about discourse structure?

One fundamental notion that has been suggested is that of an **exchange**, the smallest unit of interaction where one person says something which another person responds to. A variant on this notion is that of an **adjacency pair**, a pair of utterances that belong together such as a question and answer. This basic structure is extended with the introduction of presequences, which prepare the ground for the question, say, and inserted sequences, which can come between the question and answer. There is not general agreement about what the basic components of discourse are, and different theories incorporate different concepts.

What kind of structures should we expect to find in discourse? Will there be just a flat linear structure, with, say, a linear sequence of adjacency pairs? Barbara Grosz (1978) claims that there are hierarchical structures to be found.

That claim is made in the context of work on focus. **Focus** concerns the way we select a subset of the knowledge available in order to solve a problem. Understanding a linguistic utterance or piece of text requires the use of focus, just as many dealings with the world do.

The claim about hierarchical structure concerns the ways focus changes. The idea is that a main theme can be introduced, and thus is in focus, and then one can descend to a sub-theme, which becomes the new focus, but when that sub-theme is completed the focus may return to the main theme. Clearly there can be various sub-themes, which themselves contain sub-sub-themes and so on. Appreciating where one is in that structure may be required for the correct interpretation of various utterances.

E: *Good morning. I would like for you to reassemble the compressor.*
   ...
E: *I suggest you begin by attaching the pump to the platform.*
   ...   (other subtasks)
E: *Good. All that remains then is to attach the belt housing over to the belt housing frame.*
A: *All right. I assume the hole in the housing cover opens to the pump pulley rather than to the motor pulley.*
E: *Yes that is correct. The pump pulley also acts as a fan to cool the pump.*
A: *Fine. Thank you.*
A: *All right the belt housing cover is on and tightened down.*
   ...   (30 minutes + 60 utterances after beginning)
E: *Fine. Now let's see if it works.*

Fig 6.2 A sample dialogue

This kind of discourse structure was identified with respect to dialogues concerning tasks which were themselves structured. Fig 6.2 gives an example of Grosz's (p.246) which illustrates the importance and resilience of this kind of structure in relation to the interpretation of anaphoric pronouns.

What is striking about this is that *it* in the last utterance is not anaphorically linked to any of the noun phrases occurring shortly before it in the dialogue but rather to *the compressor*, which occurred half an hour previously. We must implicitly recognize the structure of the dialogue if we understand that reference.

Exercise 6.4

Invent a small dialogue which has a hierarchical structure which affects the interpretation of anaphoric pronouns but does not involve assembling a piece of machinery.

It is not being claimed that all dialogues have that kind of structure. In fact other dialogues were shown to have a lot looser structure with merely some grouping of utterances.

Rachel Reichman (1985) aimed to capture the hierarchical structure of ordinary conversations which were not structured by the nature of a task. She described her work as the creation of a discourse grammar.

She employs the Gricean phrase, a **conversational move** (Grice, 1975), meaning an utterance that "can begin a new communicative act serving a new discourse role" (Reichman p.21), e.g. presenting a claim, giving support to a claim, shifting a topic, resuming a preceding subject of discourse. Conversational moves have a temporal order. They are signalled by **clue words**, such as *because* for support for a claim or *anyway* for resuming a previous subject of discourse. The kind of discourse constituent that Reichman says are related in a hierarchical structure are **context spaces** and it is these that come in and out of focus in the sort of way that has already been discussed.

A context space is in part composed of a conversational move. In addition to a conversational move it has relationships to other context spaces. Thus a context space is supposed to be at a higher level of abstraction than a conversational move. But the labels for context spaces are in a similar spirit to those for conversational moves: e.g. issue, comment, narrative, support. One person's conversational turn could introduce several context spaces. On the other hand the utterances in one context space could be separated by other material. Also the utterances of more than one speaker can be part of the same context space. Consider Fig 6.3 which contains an imaginary conversation between John and two friends about the best way to get to Devon.

John: *I could take the coast route but I suppose it's best to go via London.*

friend 1:   *Don't take the coast route. The trains stop constantly.*

friend 2:   *You'll never get there.*

John: *O.K., London's the way to go, then.*

Fig 6.3 A dialogue about getting to Devon

John's two utterances form one context space, an issue context space, while the two friend's remarks form a second, a support context space. Thus the context spaces reflect the logical structure of the conversation rather than its temporal order or division into conversational turns.

A discourse grammar is supposed to describe appropriate kinds of context spaces and the relationships between them, just as a grammar in the area of syntax is supposed to establish appropriate word classes and the relationships between them. Some context spaces are independent - they can stand by themselves - while others are dependent on another context space. They do not make sense by themselves just as (normally) an adjective does not make sense without a noun to qualify.

This is the basis of the hierarchical structure: the dependent context space is subordinate in the hierarchy to the context space on which it depends. In our example, the support context space is dependent on the issue context space. Note that the hierarchy does not reflect the way a discourse can be divided into its parts and sub-parts, as the hierarchy suggested for the Grosz dialogue in Fig 6.2 does.

Reichman's model is seen as a dynamic structure in that participants in a conversation are regarded as constantly updating their models of the context spaces involved in the conversation and adjusting the specification of which are in focus. The model shows how participants can make predictions about what would be appropriate context spaces to arise next. But such predictions can be falsified, which may lead to more work to interpret the utterance. This can happen when a question is not answered but rather a remark is made which revives an earlier theme in the conversation.

Reichman's work is impressive in the degree of detail with which the general ideas have been worked out. We will not be able to do justice to that level of detail here.

Context spaces have a similar structure to frames, being constructed of a series of labelled slots. However, while the frames we have looked at embodied knowledge of the structure of a real world domain these frame-like context spaces capture the structure of a component of discourse structure. The high level slots can contain subslots and reference to other context spaces can be made in a slot.

All context spaces have certain standard slots. One is the status slot which indicates whether the context space is in the foreground or the background at that particular point in the discussion. If a support context space has been in focus but the support for the claim has been successfully rejected then the support context space goes into the background.

Another standard slot in all context spaces is the focus slot, which categorizes the constituents of the utterance into high, medium, low or zero focus. Recall a sentence mentioned early in the chapter,

John was full of excitement when he spoke to his brother.

This could be part of a context space in which John has a higher focus level than his brother. That could account for a later occurrence of his referring back to John rather than to his brother.

In addition to the various standard slots in any context space there are additional slots special to that kind of context space. An issue context space has three additional slots: CLAIM, which specifies the proposition and whether it is held to be true, not true, good or bad etc.; TOPIC; and SUPPORT context spaces, the latter having the form of a list.

It might be thought that demarcation of boundaries between context spaces, how they are related (e.g. is a certain utterance support for a previous claim?), and when one is resuming an earlier topic are of such subtlety that their recognition can not be automated in practice.

Certainly there are many difficulties here but Reichman has worked with the many words and phrases that can mark such moves. Fig 6.4 gives an example of hers in abbreviated form to give the spirit of it. (Reichman, 1985 p.40).

I remember what happened in January. I went home and I, um, was with my cousin. He's my age, I've mentioned him before. We were in his apartment and um we were talking. I just casually asked how my mother was doing, 'cause I hadn't, you know, I wasn't involved. I didn't know what was happening. And he goes,"Oh I think she's depressed." This is before she changed - She had this whole fiasco with a job. She never liked her position in her job, which was a big part of her stupid problem, that she never changed it. Oh, I didn't tell you. ...

(then there is 17 lines of digression about another incident with the mother)

... . But anyway, I went home in January and he told me she was upset.

Fig 6.4 The complexity of dialogue

Here the phrases, *Oh, I didn't tell you*, and, *But anyway*, very clearly mark the start of a digression and the resumption of the previous theme respectively.

Exercise 6.5

What other phrases can be used to signal the beginning and end of a digression?

Reichman's discourse grammar was implemented as an ATN. The states of the network represent the places where tests take place to see if a new development fits into the existing context. Arcs represent the conversational moves available. Registers represent the slots of a deep structure analysis of the conversation and are used to keep track of the dynamic processes, such as those involving focus. Actions set registers, construct and update context spaces, and supply the clue words for a conversational move.

6.5 Co-operation

A crucial feature of Reichman's work which has barely been mentioned is its basis in H.P.Grice's work on conversational implicature. This was work with a philosophical orientation which gives an outline of how a speaker can mean (and an audience can understand her to mean) something more than or different from what was literally said. The fundamental principle in the explanation is the cooperative principle, which in brief is: make your conversational contribution a cooperative one. This can be regarded as an instruction to conversational participants, but not one that is claimed to be always followed. Rather, an audience can only successfully interpret an utterance on the assumption that it is being followed.

Grice drew out the significance of the principle in terms of four kinds of maxims:

QUANTITY: give the right amount of information
QUALITY: only say what you believe and have good evidence for
RELATION: be relevant
MANNER: avoid obscurity and ambiguity and be brief and orderly

To get the spirit of the work, consider this conversation which John has at the train station,

John: *Where is the Devon train?*
Porter: *It is standing at Platform 4.*

In Grice's scheme we can say that John would take the porter to be conversationally implicating that the train standing at Platform 4 will be leaving within a reasonable period of time, not in two days' time, for example. (To conversationally implicate is to imply, in the sense that we are are examining .) The reasoning is that the porter will understand that the normal purpose of a passenger asking for the location of a train is in order to board it in expectation of its imminent departure. His reply will only be relevant to the presumed purpose if the train is expected to leave reasonably soon.

Exercise 6.6

Consider this alternative dialogue between John and the porter.
John: *Is the Devon train running late?*
Porter: *It left Paddington twenty minutes late.*

John would take the porter to be implicating that it was on its way
(and not derailed, for instance). Which of Grice's maxims is relevant
to that implicature?

Grice's work can be viewed against the background of his earlier work on
meaning in which the crucial concept was that of the speaker's communicative
intentions (Grice 1957). In the work on conversational implicature too there is
a lot that concerns the hearer's presumptions about the speaker's purposes,
knowledge and intentions.

However Reichman's work, while borrowing from Grice, explicitly leaves to
one side such notions as the speaker's intent. Rather, the approach is to
capture the objective structure of discourse. In that spirit Grice's maxims are
translated into the language of context spaces. Here is the rewriting of the
maxim of quantity:

> "In the development of a context space only specify those aspects of the
> referent being discussed that are needed for the accomplishment of the
> one specific conversational move served by this context space."
> (Reichman, 1985 p.30)

This in fact only concerns one aspect of the quantity maxim, the description of
referents, but still we can see how the restatement is leading it towards
objective features of the dialogue.

Grice's cooperative principle had already been incorporated into work on
natural language processing, notably in Jerrold Kaplan's CO-OP system
(Kaplan, 1983). This was a natural language system designed to allow a
cooperative style of interrogation of a database.

Suppose John's telephone call to the station connected him to an automated
system which allowed him to use natural language to interrogate a database
of times of train departures, delays, cancellations and so forth, such as was
mentioned at the beginning of Chapter 2. Fig 6.5 illustrates how a dialogue
might go.

John: *What trains leave from here for Devon between now and 4 p.m. today?*

system: *None.*

John: *What trains leave from here for Devon after 4 p.m. today?*

system: *None.*

John: *What trains leave from here for Devon tomorrow morning?*

system: *None.*

Fig. 6.5 A dialogue interrogating a trains database

If it turns out that no trains at all leave for Devon from that station then it would appear that the system has been most uncooperative. One of the things that the CO-OP system does is to detect false presuppositions on the enquirer's part and explicitly correct them in its response. Thus the system could have given a more helpful initial response by saying *No trains from this station go direct to Devon*.

This is certainly an improvement but the system could be more helpful by anticipating the next question. Speakers do not usually want to receive negative responses. The sort of thing that CO-OP does in this situation is provide an indirect response. The phrase *from here* could be eliminated from the question, which could then be interpreted as enquiring about routes to Devon that involve changing trains. The more helpful response might be,

Trains for London-Victoria leave at 14.34, 15.04 p.m. and 15.34 p.m., trains for Devon leave from London-Paddington at 15.00 and 16.00.

Arriving at the more general question depends on detecting the focus of the original question.

Interrogating databases is an increasing practical application area for natural language systems. An advantage of the CO-OP system is its portability; it does not depend on any particular subject domain, working as it does on general pragmatic principles. From database interrogation we could move on to reservation-making systems. The HAM-ANS system includes a hotel reservation system as well as a database system. In the HAM-ANS system there is a degree of user modelling, starting with a model of a typical user, which is supplemented with information obtained as the dialogue progresses. See McTear (1987, Ch. 8) for further description of HAM-ANS and a range of natural language systems with pragmatic relevance including the use of user modelling.

6.6 Speech acts

A topic that needs to be considered in connection with cooperation and user modelling is that of indirect speech acts. A **speech act,** or more precisely an illocutionary act, is an act which we attribute to a speaker which concerns something over and above the factual or descriptive content of an utterance. It is concerned rather with the function or role of an utterance in its communicative context. For example, a fellow passenger saying to John *A hinge on that door is loose* may well be said to be warning John about the door. It was intended as a warning and John took it that way. However in different circumstances, perhaps in the workshop, it may count merely as an act of informing.

Warning, informing, promising and requesting are just a few examples of illocutionary acts, or simply speech acts. Alarming is not included. The passenger may well have alarmed John by saying what she did, but that does not count as an illocutionary act for the production of that effect does depend on the audience recognizing an intention to produce the effect.

Some speech acts are pretty clearly indicated by the surface character of the sentence. For example the *would* interrogative form as in *Would you please close the door?* is conventionally associated with making a request. However the same intent may be expressed in the form *Can you close the door?* This is not so closely linked with the expression of a request.   Rather the conventionally indicated illocutionary act is that of a question concerning the addressee's ability to do something.

Of course, the utterance is readily enough accepted as an expression of a request, but, following Searle (1975), we should say that two speech acts have been performed. The request, which is called **the primary speech act**, has been made by means of the act of questioning the ability, which is called **the secondary speech act.**   In that case it is relatively well understood how the one speech act can be understood as the other. Having the ability to perform an action is a precondition for complying with a request to perform the action. Polite forms often avoid making a direct request of someone. A question concerning a precondition for the action is thus substituted for the explicit request.

A cooperative natural language system dealing with enquiries about train times would have to deal with indirect speech acts at least to some extent. John may say, *I want to go to Devon this afternoon*. The speech act determined by the literal meaning is the expression of a want. But the primary speech act in this context is a request for information about train times. This situation may be handled by, in effect, having a preconception of the speaker as a requester of train times and merely filling slots for destination and time.

A more subtle treatment, which would be required in a less stereotyped environment, would recognize a statement of a goal and work out what information could be supplied which is relevant to the achievement of the goal. This kind of means-end reasoning has already been mentioned in connection with plans, and will be involved in language generation in Chapter 7. Having a model of a speaker's beliefs and goals is going to be required to create a cooperative converser. It is to be hoped that indirect speech acts will be tractable in such a system.

6.7 Summary

In this chapter we have looked at some of the many ways in which single utterances need to be understood in a greater context: a context of the surrounding linguistic utterances, a context of the way the world is and a context of the speaker's presumed beliefs and goals. Thus one focus has been on the way one cannot separate knowledge of the world from the understanding of language. But another focus has been on discourse structure, which examines the logical structure of a dialogue independently of substantial knowledge of the subject area. The emphasis has been on comprehension rather than the production of appropriate utterances. However, many of the considerations mentioned here will ultimately need to be brought to bear upon language production, which is our next topic.

7

Text Generation

7.1 Generating simple texts

It should not come as a surprise that a grammar can be used to generate text. We have discussed the concept of generative grammar in Chapter 3. To date we have used our grammars for the tasks of recognizing that a sentence belongs to or fits our grammar, and for building up intermediate representations of a sentence as a tree during parsing.

Our treatment has placed heavy emphasis on these tasks and one can be led to believe that this is the purpose of a grammar. Natural language processing, however, does include the use of a grammar for the purpose of text generation. A grammar tells you when a sentence, phrase and word is grammatically (and for the last, lexically) correct. It must be possible, therefore, to reverse the process to produce grammatically (and lexically) correct words, phrases and sentences. Many of the approaches to natural language understanding have been reversed in this way; our aim in this chapter is to show how this has been done and what problems have been encountered in doing it.

Integral to the production of natural text is the construction of a representation for what we want to say. We will look at a method for achieving this, and look also at the most current techniques for determining the consequent action of working out how to say something.

In the early part of the 1960s text generation was performed to simply test a grammar for over-generation. This process gives at least a measure of how good a particular grammar is at producing meaningful sentences. It was achieved by randomly selecting among the options at each non-terminal of the grammar, starting with the S and continuing down until the words were reached.

Later systems had the benefit of more complex meaning representations (in the context of an interactive system) on which to base their generation. These included semantic networks, conceptual dependency graphs, ATNs, and so on. We will begin our treatment of text generation by showing how this can be achieved with the use of interleaving semantic markers with DCGs.

7.2 Definite clause grammars

The DCG formalism is easy to manipulate to produce text at the sentence and phrase level. Chapter 5 discussed the use of semantic markers to allow only grammatically correct and meaningful sentences. For generation purposes some form of semantic verification is essential. Consider the following grammar and lexicon taken from Chapter 5:

```
isa(john, human).
isa(sally, human).
isa(human, animate).
isa(money, phys).
isa(phys, inanimate).

really_is(X,Y) :- isa(X,Y), !.
really_is(X,Y) :- isa(X,Z), really_is(Z,Y).

v_compatible(V,N,C) :- has_vrule(V,C = X), really_is(N,X).

has_vrule(V,X) :- vrule(V,X).
has_vrule(V,X) :- isa(V,W), has_vrule(W,X).

vrule(paid, subj = human).
vrule(paid, obj = phys).
vrule(paid, obj = human).

s --> np(Subj), vp(V), { v_compatible(V,Subj,subj)}.

np(N) --> proper(N).
np(N) --> det, noun(N).

vp(V) --> verb(V), np(O), {v_compatible(V,O,obj)}.
vp(V) --> verb(V), {v_compatible(V,nil,obj)}.
```

proper(sally) --> [sally].
proper(john) --> [john].
verb(paid) --> [paid].
det --> [the].
noun(money) --> [money].

In order to generate all sentences using this grammar we ask the question

?- s(X,[]), write(X), nl, fail.

The system responses to this query are:

X = [sally, paid, sally]
X = [sally, paid, john]
X = [sally, paid, the, money]
X = [john, paid, sally]
X = [john, paid, john]
X = [john, paid, the, money]

But for the two cases where *herself* and *himself* would be more appropriate we have generated reasonable sentences from our grammar. We will return to this example when we discuss the difficulties of using this approach in Section 7.5.

7.3 Generating questions

Question-answering systems have been extremely popular and important applications for natural language processing. Many of the applications, for example expert systems, require an answer to be generated by the system from questions posed by the user. The generation problem in this case amounts to deciding how much information to provide (Allen, 1983). In other systems, such as for computer-aided learning, diagnostic expert systems or conversational systems like ELIZA (Weizenbaum, 1966), a question must be generated from some representation of what needs to be said. In this section we will look at how to achieve this when the representation is provided as a declarative sentence, perhaps from a grammar-based generator as in Section 7.1. Our focus will be on using transition networks for this purpose.

The process by which a transition network transforms an input representation into an output representation is known as transduction. The idea is to generate output symbols at the same time as processing input symbols. The transduction process can be used to perform somewhat limited machine translation, to provide an intermediate representation of the input (such as a parse tree) or to re-work input into an output form suitable for maintaining a very limited form of reflexive human-machine interaction.

Yes-no questions can be generated from statements by using transformational rules (see Exercise 3.10). We will examine the rule that transforms sentences containing only main verbs (but not *to be*) into questions. Sentences with various optional verbs before the main verb and the case where *to be* is the main verb are discussed in Exercise 7.2. You should note that very complex statements can be turned into equally complex questions. Exercise 7.3 discusses an appropriate rule for these cases.

For example,

Main verb = go

S: *John went to Devon.*
Q: *Did John go to Devon?*

Depending on the tense of the main verb an appropriate form of the verb *to do* is inserted at the front of the statement. In this case the statement is in the past tense and so the past tense of *do* (i.e. *did*) is inserted.

How then do we use a transition network to generate questions from declarative statements using the do-insertion rule? An answer to this question is provided in Fig 7.1. An input/output pair is associated with each arc. The next object in the input text is consumed provided it is of the type specified by the input parameter, and an object is produced of the type specified by the output parameter. The special symbol # indicates the null object, i.e. nothing is consumed or produced.

Only the top-level network is shown; for lower level networks, such as the **np**, **pp**, **thirdps**, and so forth, their output would simply be their input.

This solution nicely shows the limitations of using transition networks (recursive or otherwise) without memory for language analysis. We do not know until the subject and verb have been encountered whether to prefix the output with *Does* (if using the third person singular and the main verb is in the present tense), *Do* (all other present tense cases) or *Did* (when the main verb is in the past tense). The operation on the main verb is always the same: we output its infinitive form, but we need to note its tense, etc. when traversing the verb arc and store the appropriate form of *do* at that stage. An augmented transition network has precisely this ability. Check the responses generated by the network when processing the following sentences as input:

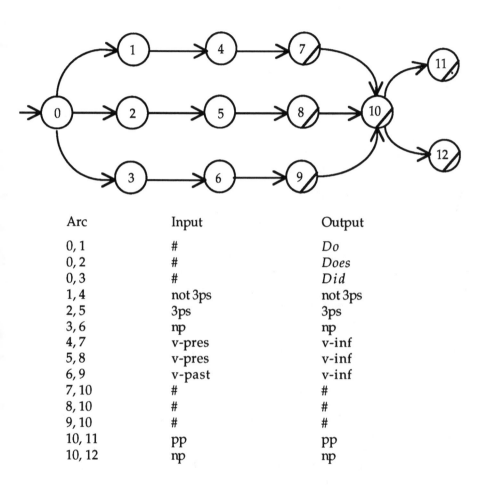

Arc	Input	Output
0, 1	#	Do
0, 2	#	Does
0, 3	#	Did
1, 4	not 3ps	not 3ps
2, 5	3ps	3ps
3, 6	np	np
4, 7	v-pres	v-inf
5, 8	v-pres	v-inf
6, 9	v-past	v-inf
7, 10	#	#
8, 10	#	#
9, 10	#	#
10, 11	pp	pp
10, 12	np	np

Fig 7.1 S-to-Q network

John went to Devon.
He likes aunt Betty.
They went on the train.

Questions are not limited to obtaining only *yes-no* responses. Depending on the information contained in the statement more detailed responses can be requested. Questions can be asked using: *Which, Where, Who, What, When, Why* and *How*. These questions are collectively known as *wh*-questions. The transformations associated with each of these are fairly complicated

(Akmajian and Heny, 1979). We will make some broad assumptions which will cover all cases.

An initial classification of the different types of *wh*-questions can be made based on a parts of speech analysis of each. *Which* and *what* have the role of determiners in questions, as in

S: *That train goes to Devon.*
Q: *Which train does go to Devon?*

S: *The birds annoyed him.*
Q: *What birds did annoy him?*

S: *John woke to the sound of birds.*
Q: *What did John wake to?*

What is somewhat special as it can function as a complete noun phrase, as in the last example above (and also in *What did annoy him?*). Note also that there are alternative ways of asking these questions. In these examples our generated questions seem somewhat strange and have an emphatic character to them.

We could simply swap the determiner with the *wh*-word, as in

What train goes to Devon?,
What birds annoyed him?

to produce more natural sounding questions. These are cases where the determiners are in the subject noun phrase. We are trying to cover as many possible cases as we can with our rule, but because there are many ways of asking the same question we have to accept that our rule will not generate the most natural sounding question in all circumstances.

For *who* and sometimes *what* (and unfortunately *which* also) we can say that they perform the role of noun phrases:

S: *John went to Devon.*
Q: *Who did go to Devon?*

S: *The train went to Devon.*
Q: *What did go to Devon?*

Clearly, we do make further semantic distinctions when forming these questions. *Who* is linked with an animate noun phrase and *what* with an inanimate one.

The other *wh*-questions are grouped together as words that perform specific roles in various referring expressions. *Where* refers to a place; *when* to time; *why* to reason and *how* to a description of a manner or means of doing something. The expressions are typically adjectives, adverbs or prepositional phrases. We will use the generic term *wh*-phrase to cover the phrase in the sentence which the *wh*-word refers to. Finally, it should be noted that this phrase contains the answer to the generated question, an issue discussed later in the context of ongoing discourse.

The following (where the *wh*-phrase does not refer to the subject noun phrase) sound much more natural:

S: *John went to Devon.*
Q: *Where did John go?*

S: *John went immediately.*
Q: *When did John go?*

S: *John went because he had to.*
Q: *Why did John go?*

S: *John went to Devon by train.*
Q: *How did John go to Devon?*

The transformational rules we are using here take the original sentence and initially perform a transformation to a *yes/no* question. Here all the examples involve a main verb; you should check that the method holds for auxiliary verbs too (see Exercise 7.2). The final transformation is to move the *wh*-phrase to the front of the *yes/no* question. Thus,

John went to Devon by train.

Did John go to Devon by train?   { by yes/no rule }
                    wh-phrase = PP

How did John go to Devon?

Exercise 7.1

Add register manipulations to the transition network diagram to achieve sentence to question transduction.

Exercise 7.2

The second yes-no transformational rule is embodied in the following examples, and relates to situations where the statement contains an optional modal auxiliary verb (in our grammar, MODAL), or other auxiliary verbs (HAVE or BE), or if none of the previous options hold, where the main verb is *be*.

Auxiliary :

Modal	S:	*John may go to Devon.*
	Q:	*May John go to Devon?*
Progressive	S:	*John is going to Devon.*
	Q:	*Is John going to Devon?*
Perfect	S:	*John has gone to Devon.*
	Q:	*Has John gone to Devon?*
Main verb = *be*	S:	*John is excited.*
	Q:	*Is John excited?*

The rule for moving from S to Q is simply to swap the auxiliary (or other options) with the subject noun phrase of the statement. Write down an ATN to deal with this case. Try to develop a network to deal with *wh*-questions for this case.

Exercise 7.3

Exercise 7.2 can be extended to cover the generation of negative statements

Modal	S:	*John may go to Devon.*
	N:	*John may not go to Devon.*
Progressive	S:	*John is going to Devon.*
	N:	*John isn't going to Devon.*
Perfect	S:	*John has gone to Devon.*
	N:	*John hasn't gone to Devon.*
Main verb = *be*	S:	*John is in Devon.*
	N:	*John isn't in Devon.*

Develop an ATN solution to this problem and include the main-verb case.

Exercise 7.4

If you have solved 7.3 try to generate negative reaction or confirmation questions, for example:
   S: *John is going to Devon.*
   N: *John isn't going to Devon.*
   NQ: *Isn't John going to Devon?*

Exercise 7.5

Write an ATN which uses the *yes/no* ATN to perform *wh*-question generation. Try to include the generation of negative questions in your network.

Exercise 7.6

Consider the following facts that could be expressed as a semantic network:

   isa('Devon',county).
   location('Devon','South_West_England').
   isa(county,'Division_of_England').
   number_of('Division_of_England',46).

How would you use this network to produce natural responses to questions such as:

   What is Devon?
   Where is Devon?
   What is a county?

7.4 Template-based approaches

One of the simplest methods for generating text in the context of providing a response to some input, rather than in, say, generating a story, is to reflect most of the input back to the user in the response. The technique of reflective questioning which results is a technique sometimes practised by counsellors, psychoanalysts, doctors, and so forth. It can lead to remarkably sensible dialogues. When implemented as an interactive dialogue between machine and human, the human subject can be easily misled into believing that they are conversing with something that is actually listening to what they are saying. The most famous example of this is Joseph Weizenbaum's ELIZA program (Weizenbaum 1966).

The technique may be loosely termed a slot and filler template system. Templates (sentences and phrases) are prepared in advance with empty slots. During a conversation, if a phrase matches the prepared template then the slot will be filled from the input and another prepared output phrase containing the filled slot will be used to echo a response. Consider, for example, the following input and output templates:

input	output
(I am ____)	(What makes you think you are ____ ?)
(____body ____ me)	(____body ____ you?)
(No *)	(Why not?)

In the last entry the asterisk will match anything, so (No *) means that any input after No is ignored. Here are some interactions:

subject>	I am crazy.
machine>	What makes you think you are crazy?
subject>	Nobody loves me.
machine>	Nobody loves you?
subject>	No.
machine>	Why not?

Of course this can generate some strange conversations:

subject>	I am back.
machine>	What makes you think you are back?
subject>	Everybody knows me.
machine>	Everybody knows you?
subject>	No not exactly everybody.
machine>	Why not?

A finite state or pushdown (RTN) transducer can be readily adapted to this task (Gazdar and Mellish, 1989).

This technique is somewhat open to abuse in a very general context but when things become more specific, as in the blocks world (Winograd, 1972), it can be used for answering *how* and *why* type questions quite naturally.

Many expert systems use some form of prepared (or canned) response to give explanatory responses to a user's question. Because of the restricted domain, it is decided in advance that the *how* and *why* questions refer back to the internal knowledge representation of the system.

The explanation facility will search through a decision tree constructed from the knowledge base at run-time. The explanation makes use of a data structure of nodes visited by the system when it attempts to solve a problem. For *why* queries, the data structure is displayed from the current node back to the root node of the decision tree. *Why* explanations give rule application information. A typical *why*-explanation (Bratko, 1990) is given below. The original question is *john is-visiting aunt?* and the current node is *john packed suitcase*.

[(john is_on holiday) via rule23, (john is_visiting aunt) via rule17]

If I can establish john packed suitcase then
I can investigate john is_on holiday via rule23 then
Finally, I can solve john is_visiting aunt via rule17
and john is_visiting aunt was your original question.

This can be accomplished with the following code:

```
:- op(100,xfx,via).

start_to_explain(Current_Node) :-
        nl, write('If I can establish '),
        write(Current_Node), write(' then').

explain_history([Root_Node via Rule]) :-
        nl, write('Finally, I can solve '), write(Root_Node via Rule),
        nl, write('and '), write(Root_Node),
        write(' was your original question').

explain_history([Node1 via Rule1, Node2 via Rule2 | Rest]) :-
        nl, write('I can investigate '), write(Node1 via Rule1),
        write(' then'), explain_history([ Node2 via Rule2 | Rest]).
```

For *how* queries a similar data structure of nodes is displayed but this time from the root node to the current node. *How* explanations provide information on the deductions the system made during the problem-solving process. An overview of expert system explanation facilities is given in Rolston (1988).

7.5 Problems with simple approaches

All of the approaches to generating text that we have discussed so far have their problems. Using a DCG with semantic markers produces uneven results. The constraints placed on phrase formation by the markers help, but these can easily be too general, as we saw in Section 5.6.

In this section we will look at some of the problems in generating natural looking (and sounding) text. The next section looks at ways to overcome some of these problems.

One way of producing more natural text is to use pronouns instead of proper names or nouns in noun phrases. The following text, for example, is somewhat dry:

> *John was going to Devon by train. John loved Devon.*

It could be improved by making pronoun references in the second sentence,

> *John was going to Devon by train. He loved it.*

This is now more natural sounding but is ambiguous. One of the main differences between understanding text and generating it is that we should not have to worry about ambiguity; even if there are twenty ways to say the same thing for generation purposes just one will do. If anaphoric references are to be used then it must be checked that we are not introducing ambiguity.

This problem is not restricted to inanimate nouns (see Section 6.1). Consider the ambiguity introduced by the pronoun *she* in the text

> *Joan went with her mother, sister and aunt. She is very timid you know.*

The SHRDLU system (Winograd 1983) had an interesting approach to this problem. It generated pronouns for noun phrases, deciding when to do so by using a heuristic rule. Given its limited domain of discourse it could look back at previous answers, select noun phrases that had been mentioned and insert pronouns in their places. It achieved this by defining procedures for each pronoun type that acted as an expert antecedent finder.

This seems quite a good method when you consider pronoun use in conversation. Pronouns are often used because you become tired of saying the same thing over again.   For emphasis the referent may reappear, however.   For lengthy interactions your short-term memory can only store so many pronouns so you certainly have to be careful how you use them.

The template approaches are extremely successful in their limited domains of discourse. The text they generate is sometimes stylized and awkward but sufficient for someone interacting with a program to be presented with understandable text. The key to these approaches is the restricted domain and only needing to respond to a sentence in isolation. These restrictions may be considered to be features of the approach, but in the longer term will not help to provide more natural and relevant information to a user of a system.

Their main disadvantage is that they are static, *a priori* methods. They have almost no ability to change what they are saying during an interactive session, have almost no memory of previous statements, have no knowledge of the user and no understanding of the context of the conversation. Their success crucially depends on the interactions in the discourse being completely independent of each other, which is not a terribly reliable assumption.

Further, they do not address some of the fundamental issues in text generation. Kathleen McKeown states these issues by asking the following questions of a system:

(a)   How can it determine what it should say?
(b)   How can it communicate its intent?
(c)   How can it determine the phrasing of a response?
(d)   How can it organize its response?

The degree of difficulty of each of these will, of course, be tempered by the application. *What should be said?* is extremely difficult if the system is to generate original, meaningful and interesting stories, and somewhat easier if the system is to respond to a question where at least the input is at hand.

Moreover, when holding a conversation intended to provide someone with information, a speaker takes into account the listener's knowledge of that information to decide what to say. If they are already an expert then the information may be better presented in a general and reasonably abstract manner. Completely new information, on the other hand, might best be presented in a more specific manner and backed up with examples and analogies.

Systems that provide guidance for a knowledgeable technician to, say, maintain a computer disc must have strategies for resolving situations where the instructee becomes stuck. Gauging a person's knowledge and beliefs in the course of a dialogue is a (completely) non-trivial task, but some form of user modelling would clearly aid the system in deciding what to say.

These questions can be characterized as being either **strategic** (i.e. question (a) above) or **tactical** (i.e. questions (b)-(d)). How much information the system has to deal with on the strategic question clearly depends on the application. The tactical questions can draw on grammatical, semantic and pragmatic information regardless of the application.

Exercise 7.7

How might you decide how and when to introduce an anaphoric reference?

7.6 Phrasal lexicons and the use of idioms

One of the ways in which sentences can be made to sound more natural is by replacing words with whole phrases that have the same meaning. For example by using idioms,

> *His drink was free* --> *His drink was on the house*

Restraint must be used however; *free* can be an adjective, adverb (but more usually with *freely*) or verb, and is used differently within each category. Even another instance of the same word in the same syntactic category can lead to meaningless phrases.

> *the bathroom is free* --> * *the bathroom is on the house*
> *John tried to free the people* --> * *John tried to on the house the people*

Idioms are not the only phrases that can be used. In a certain setting people tend to develop a use of language in which certain fixed phrases are commonly used, often using jargon and standard expressions. Often the technique is used to make a sentence more complex than it need be, perhaps to impress, or obfuscate:

> *Our analysis of scenarios of the future lead us to semantically ambiguous conclusions about underdetermined upcoming events.*

instead of

We do not know what is going to happen

Phrasal lexicons are dictionaries expressing these types of equivalences. One of the primary uses of these lexicons is to aid the representation of heavily hyphenated expressions, as in *means_of_travel*. A phrasal lexicon may not store the lexical and syntactic entries that would produce this phrase, it can be stored as a single entry. Frame, expert and planning systems are all good examples of where such hyphenation is often necessary.

In restricted contexts this technique can produce surprisingly good results (Kukich, 1983). Below (Exercise 7.8) is an example of the kind of text that could be produced using a phrasal lexicon.

Exercise 7.8

Try to generate a phrasal lexicon for the following example.

Rush hour services into Paddington were running late again this morning. A BR spokesperson said that the delays were due to circumstances beyond their control. The Opposition complained that the travelling public were paying the price for classic underinvestment in public services.

You should ask yourself, what fixed phrases have been used in the construction of the summary and what words might they have replaced?

7.7 Generators with greater power

Much of the work to generate natural language draws heavily from approaches taken to solve natural language understanding problems where more than one sentence is involved. The approach we will concentrate on in this section is planning, as it is at the heart of natural language generation.

It seems reasonable to use a planning approach to language generation. Before saying or writing anything it is generally wise to plan what to say or write as carefully as you can. We may ask two questions about the use of a plan for language generation. What is the state space (in particular the initial and final states)? What are the actions, preconditions and effects which influence state transitions?

Given that conversations are conducted for a myriad of different purposes, these questions are extremely difficult to address in very general terms. Some form of constraint on the purpose of the conversation has typically been applied. The KAMP system (Appelt, 1985), for example, assumes that the interaction between its users is co-operative (a robot telling a human how to assemble a water pump). A further assumption of mutually known knowledge also helps in planning sentences. These assumptions help to place constraints on the beliefs of the participants involved in the conversation. Otherwise many universal truths about beliefs and what is mutually and generally known have to be assumed.

Let us consider an example of how a planning system can help in making decisions about what to say. Much of the notation used here is taken form Gazdar & Mellish (1989) whose work is based on the original work of Philip Cohen (for example, Cohen & Perrault, 1979).

Going back to our story, we will consider the interaction between John and his mother prior to his departure to Devon to visit his aunt. John must plan what to say to his mother so that he can go on the trip.

The initial state of affairs, which must be unconditionally true for anything to happen at all, is that:

1. John and his mother can communicate with each other (i.e. they are within earshot);

2. John wants to inform his mother that he wants to go to visit his aunt in Devon.

The final state corresponds to John's receiving permission to go to Devon to visit his aunt.

The representation for initial states chosen here is a list of known facts between the person speaking and the person spoken to. The final state has just a single argument containing the information that we want to be true:

```
initial([ can_communicate(john, mother),
          can_communicate(mother, john),
          wants(john, ask_permission(john, mother, togoto_devon))])

final([   allowed(john, togoto_devon)]).
```

The actions in a plan of this form are general procedures (one can think of them as cause-effect rules) that have constraints or preconditions that must be satisfied before they can be executed (or fired). The result of an action being carried out is to make the effects of the action true (or false).

Without elaborating too much on a general set of actions let us look at some applicable actions for our example. Clearly, John must inform his mother of his intention to go:

Action:
    ask_permission(Asker, Person_Asked, Question)

Preconditions:
    can_communicate(Asker, Person_Asked)
    wants(Asker, ask_permission(Asker, Person_Asked, Question))

Effects:
    asked(Asker, Person_Asked, Question)

The preconditions can be universally held truths, truths established in previous states (such as the initial state) or the effects of performing other actions.

Asking permission is an action that demands a response. In this case the response is a permitting action:

Action:
    permit(Permitter, Permittee, To_Do_Something)

Preconditions:
    asked(Permittee, Permitter, To_Do_Something)
    good_reason(Permittee, To_Do_Something)

Effects:
    allowed(Permittee, To_Do_Something)

One way to implement a scheme which generates a plan based on the initial and final states and on actions such as those above is to treat the problem as a backward-chaining expert system. The final state is the goal to be achieved. The system moves backward from this state via its actions (rules) until it reaches the initial state. If there are no unknowns (variables) at that point the system can then unfold its plan by retracing through the actions that proved successful, much like the way we saw that a *why* query was answered.

In our example, we want the goal

allowed(john, togoto_devon)

to be true. We must search to find an action which has this goal as its effect and then try to satisfy that action's preconditions. The *permit* action is satisfied as long as

asked(john, mother, togoto_devon) &
good_reason(john, togoto_devon)

are true. The second precondition can be treated here, somewhat loosely, as an example of a universal truth, namely that everyone always has good reasons for doing something.

Since the first precondition is the effect of another action it is treated as our new goal and we repeat the procedure again. The *asked* condition will be true in our *ask_permission* action since all its preconditions are satisfied in the initial state.

The plan the system comes up with is for John to ask his mother to allow him to go by requesting her permission. The plan is created as a list of actions to be performed in order.

1.   ask_permission(john, mother, togoto_devon)
2.   permit(mother, john, togoto_devon)

What we have achieved with our plan this far is an idea of what to say, how to organize what we want to say, and to a lesser extent how to say it. The plan provides us with illocutionary information i.e. the information that is unsaid prior to actually forming an appropriate surface form for a sentence (see Section 6.6). We know that John must ask his mother by making a request for permission to go on the trip, as opposed, say, to making a suggestion or a statement. The plan as it stands, however, does not tell us what John should actually say. This can be achieved by using a template approach as in Section 7.4 or by taking the planning paradigm further and adopting a multi-layered planning approach.

In general, achieving a goal may be subtly dependent on how we phrase our utterances. Given the task *ask_permission(john, mother, togoto_devon)*, John has some choices to make. He can ask his mother for permission using different sentential structures, for example:

Declaratively   - e.g. *I am going to Devon, if that's alright with you.*
Interrogatively   - e.g. *May I go to Devon?*
Imperatively   - e.g. *Give me permission to go to Devon!*

All of these would do the job, and depending on John's degree of *want* will be stressed in different ways. The imperative form seems totally inappropriate in the context of asking permission as it seems to be more of a demand than a request.

The declarative form seems appropriate for an older person who is asking for permission to go, but only in the sense that there might be something else his mother wants him to do. The implication is *I am going to Devon; I will not go only if there is something (presumably urgent) that will prevent me from doing so.* Given that John is on his school holidays it might be appropriate to use our knowledge of the speaker to rule this case out. This leaves us to generate the interrogative form. This example only reinforces the difficulty systems face in generating text.

We have now descended to a new level of analysis. We have worked out from the illocutionary plan that a request is needed. Our present analysis is at the sentence level and we have decided to use the interrogative form. Our analysis attempts to plan the actual utterance by using the actions generated by the illocutionary plan. We plan to use an interrogative sentential form, say, MODAL NP VP, and then try to realize this form by planning the MODAL, the NP and the VP, via the actions that are generated by the illocutionary plan. Each of these plans can be thought of as a planning layer, the overall system comprising a hierarchy of such layers.

The layer for realizing a modal form would have preconditions that checked to see which modal is most appropriate. These conditions may not be distinguishable until other layers have been traversed. Planning systems often have the ability to make decisions to change the planned utterance as more information becomes available. This is the case in the KAMP system. The TEXT system (McKeown, 1985) has a strict hierarchy; no layer can influence any of the other layers.

Typical actions for noun phrases would be to make referring expression decisions such as pronoun selection (*I go ...*) and non-pronoun selection (*the clerk, that man*), ensuring number agreement, etc. Verb phrases would contain information on the use of the verbs with preconditions to perform checks on the verb usage, check number agreement with the subject noun phrase, and so forth.

At the word level there is the opportunity to perform morphological analysis, and to use more natural sounding expressions such as *that's his, haven't you*

finished and also to include punctuation *John's aunt, a lovely lady, was ....*
Returning to our example let us assume that the modal *may* has been chosen as
being most appropriate.

The NP layer must decide on an appropriate phrase. As John is doing the
wanting we know that he is referring to himself, suggesting the personal
pronoun *I* for the subject of the sentence. If this is chosen the tense of the main
verb must be first person singular, which places a precondition on the
generated verb in the VP. The representation of the question does not
immediately indicate the verb, but we will assume that *go* can be extracted.
This representation demands the use of a phrasal lexicon so that the verb can
be extracted from the phrase and then modified appropriately.

An interesting choice arises with the selection of the verb. If we choose the
intransitive form we can generate

   May I go?

which (presumably) would work but only after his mother had asked him
where he wanted to go to. Given that we have placed more information in the
illocutionary plan we know in advance that an indirect object is needed and
that a prepositional phrase will provide it. Thus, a precondition of a *go*
action would be to have an indirect object to act on.

This example is intended to give an idea of the process of planning an
utterance. Many of the details have been either assumed or glossed over. We
have not, for example, included any analysis of John and his mother's beliefs,
or knowledge that they mutually share. For example, John can ask to go to
Devon and omit the TO-PHRASE (*to visit aunty*) if he and his mother know
that that is the only reason why John would go to Devon.

Exercise 7.9

Describe the difference between the context in which you use *can* and
the context in which you use *may*. Think of suitable preconditions
that would serve to differentiate the two contexts (see Section 6.6 on
speech acts).

7.8 Grammars for text generation

We have seen how transition networks can be used to drive text generation. The ATN is superior to other finite state approaches owing to its ability to store values in registers as it processes the input. The benefits over the other network approaches are that there is less non-determinism and that transformational rules can be implemented. When we try to embed an ATN in a multi-module system which uses other knowledge sources (such as previous interactions, user model, and so on) to work out a response, the ATN proves to be too inflexible a partner. It will make decisions about the form of the sentence which cannot be reversed without re-iterating the process.

A more flexible approach allowing many choices to be made about the type of sentence to be produced is afforded by systemic grammars (Halliday & Martin, 1981). One particular system, PROTEUS, due to Davey (1979) generates descriptions of games of noughts and crosses. Although a very early system it is perceived to be one of the best. Here is an example of the text it can generate.

I threatened you by taking the middle of the edge opposite that and adjacent to the one I had just taken but you blocked it and threatened me.

Systemic grammars emphasize the functional organization of language. It does this by defining a number of choice systems and represents these as a system network, a kind of and/or graph (see Fig 7.2). Vertical bars indicate disjunction while braces indicate conjunction. The choice systems embody the meaningful options that a speaker has when constructing words, phrases and sentences. The expressions in Fig 7.2 that are prefixed by operators will be explained later.

The choices reflect the available **features** in the system. At the lexical level these features are the traditional alternatives, such as singular or plural, masculine or feminine, animate or inanimate. Higher level features reflect other attributes of language, such as active or passive, declarative or imperative.

As well as providing feature choices the system also encodes functional roles played by a particular feature such as subject and object. We have seen these roles before in our discussion of case grammars in Chapter 5. Systemic grammars are quite closely related to case grammars (Winograd, 1983).

Given that we have different ways of analysing a sentence in terms of a functional or feature description how do we integrate the two into the system and how do we use the result for generation purposes?

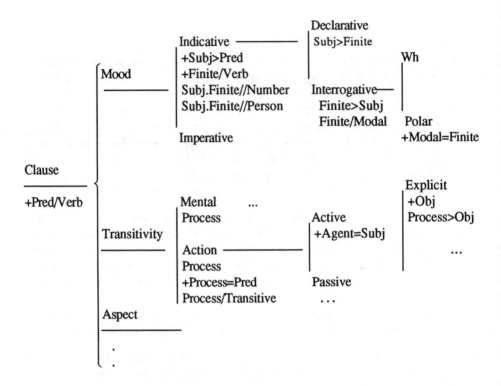

Fig 7.2 Systemic grammar

Rule	Action	Operator
Inclusion	adds all functions to a feature	+
Conflation	assigns a function to another	=
Classification	classifies a feature with a function	/
Ordering	states which function appears before another	>
Agreement	for a particular system, checks a function with another to see if they agree	//

Fig 7.3 Realization Rules

The integration and, to a large extent, the generation is accomplished through **realization** rules. Each choice system, through its features and functions, imposes some constraint on the final form of the sentence. The realization rules provide a mechanism for relating and manipulating these constraints. The rules are stated in Fig 7.3.

The network represented in Fig 7.2 contains some very general examples of these rules which are executed during the generation phase. They state, for example, that every clause (which is essentially a sentence) must have a verb functioning as a predicate (inclusion); that indicative clauses must have a subject which precedes the predicate (ordering); that the finite element will be a verb carrying number, tense and person (classification); that the finite element will agree in person and number with the subject (agreement); and so on.

The algorithm for generating sentences uses these rules; the process is indicated in the following example. Consider the planning example of Section 7.7 where the content of the utterance has been decided by the illocutionary planner but the sentence realization has been left to a systemic grammar.

The planner asks the grammar for a request. The grammar immediately generates a [Clause] feature. Entering the **Clause** system we must choose (owing to the **and** bracket) a feature from each of the systems **Mood**, **Transitivity**, **Aspect**, and so on. It should be noted that **Transitivity** does not simply imply transitive or intransitive verb, it defines through the main verb the process or relationship aspects of a sentence. This could involve one or more noun phrases (for direct and indirect objects, etc.).

Given that we have a request, the [Indicative] feature is chosen and then the [Interrogative] and [Polar] (corresponding to a question where the response is polarized, i.e. *yes* or *no*). From the **Transitivity** system other features will be generated, [Action] then [Active] and finally [Explicit].

Without going into too many details, and making some simplifications, we arrive at a list of features for our sentence, with some of the choices being determined by the content planner,

[Clause, Indicative, Interrogative, Polar, Action, Active, Explicit]

Once the features have been chosen their associated realization rules can be applied. Following Winograd we tabulate this process in Fig 7.4. You should work through the process using the network in Fig 7.2 as a guide.

Feature	Rules	Result
Inclusion		
Clause	+Pred	
Indicative	+Subj, +Finite	
Polar	+Modal	
Action	+Process	
Active	+Agent	
Explicit	+Object	Pred Subj Finite Modal
		Process Agent Object
Conflation		
Polar	Finite = Modal	
Action	Process = Pred	
Active	Agent = Subject	Pred.Process Subj.Agent
		Finite.Modal Object
Classification		
Clause	Pred/Verb	Pred.Process(Verb Transitive)
Indicative	Finite/Verb	Subj.Agent()
Interrogative	Finite/Modal	Finite.Modal (Verb Modal)
Action	Process/Transitive	Object()
Fill constituents		
	Dictionary	Pred.Process - go
		(Verb Present singular Transitive)
	NP network	Subj.Agent - I
		(NP personal singular first)
	Dictionary	Finite.Modal - May
		(Verb Modal)
	PP network	Object - to Devon
		(PP Prep NP (place-name))
Ordering		
Indicative	Subj > Pred	I go
Interrogative	Finite > Subj	May I go
Explicit	Process > Obj	May I go to Devon
Agreement		
Indicative	Subj,Finite//Person	ok
	Subj,Finite//Number	ok

Fig 7.4 The application of realization rules

The systemic grammar approach embraces the notions of setting preconditions, checking agreements, and providing order, allowing a functional analysis to be performed at the same time. The most comprehensive treatment of systemic grammar can be found in the NIGEL system of Mann & Matthiessen (1985).

For generation purposes the main problem is selecting a suitable feature set. The integration of the planning component and the systemic grammar is far from obvious, especially if we want to allow the integration to affect any of the choice systems in the system network. Mann and Matthiessen have developed a technique to do this.

Exercise 7.10

Generate some other sentences using the systemic grammar in Fig 7.2. Work out why the precedence relations are within one choice system and not another. What rules would you add for *wh* - questions?

7.9 Functional unification grammar

Given that we want a system that performs both natural language understanding and generation it would be useful if they could be performed by one system, rather than say having an ATN for input and a systemic grammar for output. In this circumstance two entirely different representations and control mechanisms would have to be implemented.

One approach to developing such reversibility is taken in **functional unification grammar**. It is functional because it contains and manipulates those elements that perform functional roles in language, as in case and systemic grammars, such as agent, theme, and the like. The functional elements have not, as yet, been employed extensively in this formalism. The term unification is the process described in Section 4.9, and it is this process that controls generation.

To generate output using a FUG, we supply an initial functional description (derived from some planning scheme) and then use unification to successively merge this description with the grammar. The best way to view this process is to follow through an example. We will just consider the top-level sentence rule that applies to our example; in a real FUG there would be many alternatives to explore. We will use the same notation as in Chapter 4 and the same roles as per the systemic grammar example above.

The following rule contains a number of slots to be filled (via the assignment statement).

```
[ (finite subject predicate object)
  cat = s
  tense = present
  subject = actor = [ cat = np ]
  voice = active
  predicate = [   cat = verb
                  transitivity = action
                  voice = active ]
  object =      {[  cat = np ]
                 [  cat = pp ]} ]
```

It is unified with the various phrase and lexical rules, such as

```
[ (prep np)            [ (proper)            [ (pronoun)
  cat = pp               cat = np ]            cat = np ]
  object = np ]

[ cat = proper         [ cat = pronoun
  word = 'Devon' ]       case = subjective
                         number = singular
                         person = first
                         word = 'I' ]
```

to produce

```
[ (finite subject predicate object)
  cat = s
  tense = present
  finite = [   cat = verb
               word = may ]
  subject = actor = np = [   cat = pronoun
                             case = subjective
                             number = singular
                             person = first
                             word = 'I' ]
  voice = active
  predicate = [ [   cat = verb
                    word = go ]
                transitivity = action
                voice = active ]
  object = [   cat = pp
               prep = [   cat = preposition
               word = to ]
               np  = [   cat = proper
                    word = 'Devon' ]  ] ]
```

Fig 7.5 Generation of a sentence using FUG

The main advantage of this approach over others is the union of syntactic, semantic and pragmatic information in one notation which is governed by one control process. There are computational problems associated with using unification as a control process; the exploration of many alternatives in a grammar is extremely inefficient. The process also suffers from a standard problem with rule-based systems of deciding which rule to fire when the conditions of several rules have been satisfied. The properties of reversibility and notational consistency, however, are so attractive that many systems (such as KAMP and TEXT) have been developed using this technique.

7.10 Summary

We have only given a flavour of this very rich and diverse field of endeavour. For example, the interested reader might like to consider how the conceptual dependency grammar developed in Chapter 5 might be used to generate a question such as *May I go to Devon?*

An excellent summary of research in the field of text generation is given by McDonald (1987), including his view of the state of the art. We have not the scope or space to include all the systems and all the techniques that have been used to successfully generate text.

Current systems are tackling some of the very hard problems of this area. There is general agreement that a text generation system must decide what to say and how to say it. We know further that for discourse purposes we need to have a model of the user, have some understanding of what they know, what is mutually understood and what is generally understood.

Text generation has, according to many authors, taken a back seat to its supposed counterpart, natural language understanding. This situation is due in part to the belief that text generation is simply the inverse of understanding. Hopefully, this chapter will have gone some way to convince you otherwise.

Solutions to Exercises

Chapter 2

Exercise 2.1

Here is the phonemic transcription of the second and third sentences:

It was the first day of his summer holidays and he was going to stay
with his aunt   who lived in Devon.
/ɪt/ /wɒz/ /ðə/ /fɜːst/ /deɪ/ /aʊv/ /hɪz/ /sʌmər/ /hɒlɪdeɪs/
/ænd/ /hiː/ /wɒz/ /ɡaʊɪŋ/ /tə/ /steɪ//wɪð/ /hɪz/ /ɑːnt/
/huː/ /lɪvd/ /ɪn/ /devən/

Visiting aunts can be fun so he rang the station to discover the times of
trains.
/vɪzɪtɪŋ/ /ɑːnts/ /kæn/ /biː/ /fʌn/ /saʊ/ /hiː//ræŋ/ /ðə/
/steɪʃən/ /tə/ /dɪskʌvər/ /ðə//taɪms/ /aʊv/ /treɪns/

Exercise 2.2

bigger	= *bigg - er*
enormous	= *e - norm - ous*
gamekeeper	= *game - keep - er*
illegitimate	= *il - legit - im - ate*
itemize	= *item - ize*
lights	= *light - s*
she'll	= *she - 'll*
smallest	= *small - est*
synchronization	= *syn - chron - iz - ation*
trainee	= *train - ee*

Exercise 2.3

There are many examples; here are three:

> *rasp* in *raspberry*
> *scrut* in *inscrutable*
> *wor* in *worship*

Exercise 2.4

a) There are many examples; here are two:

> *ox --> oxen*
> *terminus --> termini*

b) The plural of *fish* is **both** *fish* and *fishes*.

Exercise 2.5

derivational:

able	excite (N)	->	excitable (Adj)
a l	spectre (N)	->	spectral (Adj)
ance	ally (V)	->	alliance (N)
ate	origin (N)	->	originate (V)
ation	note(V)	->	notation (N)
cy	supreme (Adj)	->	supremacy (N)
ence	defer (V)	->	deference (N)
er	walk (V)	->	walker (N)
hood	likely (Adj)	->	likelihood (N)
ible	divide (V)	->	divisible (Adj)
iful	beauty (N)	->	beautiful (Adj)
ion	divide (V)	->	division (N)
ish	boy (N)	->	boyish (Adj)
ise/ize	legal (Adj)	->	legalize (V)
ist	legal (Adj)	->	legalist (N)
ity	legal (Adj)	->	legality (N)
less	hope (N)	->	hopeless (Adj)
like	crab (N)	->	crablike (Adj)
ly	proper (Adj)	->	properly (Advb)
ment	govern (V)	->	government (N)
ness	thorough (Adj)	->	thoroughness (N)
ous	wonder(V)	->	wondrous(Adj)
some	loathe (V)	->	loathsome (Adj)
ster	young (Adj)	->	youngster (N)
ward	home (N)	->	homeward (Adj)
wise	clock (N)	->	clockwise (Adj)

inflectional:

age	bag (N)	->	baggage (N)
dom	king (N)	->	kingdom (N)
ed	walk (V)	->	walked (V + past)
en	take (V)	->	taken (V + en)
ery	pig (N)	->	piggery (N)
est	large (Adj)	->	largest (Adj + super)
ing	divide (V-inf)	->	dividing (V-ing)
's	cow(N)	->	cow's (N +poss)
s'	cow(N)	->	cows' (N +poss)
s	cow(N)	->	cows (N +plur)
ship	friend (N)	->	friendship (N)
teen	six (Adj)	->	sixteen (Adj)
ty	six (Adj)	->	sixty (Adj)
way	air (N)	->	airway (N)

Exercise 2.6

Nouns:	*bedroom*	*washing-up*	*backpack*
	greatcoat	*bulldog*	*throughput*
	hit-man		

Verbs:	*backpack*	*oversee*	*wash-up*

Adjective:	*freestyle*	*stone-cold*	*undercover*

Rule1: if second component is v-inf, then result is v-inf.
Rule 2: if second component is noun, then result is noun.
Exception: where one of the components is a preposition.

Exercise 2.7

Add to Figs 2.6 & 2.7:

```
spell_check(Word) :- dict(Word), !.
spell_check(Word) :- plural_noun(Root, Word), dict(Root, noun), !.

% similarly for other inflectional checking routines,
% e.g. spell_check(Word) :-
%         past_tense(Root, Word), dict(Root, verb), !.

sibilant(X) :- member(X, [s, x, sh, z, ch]).
```

```
dict(child, noun).
dict(crazy, adj).
dict(station, noun).
dict(baby, noun).
dict(church, noun).
```

Exercise 2.8

NOUN ::=	aunt I bird I bus I can I clerk I day I delay I fun I holiday I house I left I locomotive I luggage I mother I other I sound I station I stop I summer I time I train
V-INF ::=	as before + board I break I live I cancel I decide I pass I run I ring I tell I visit I wake
V-PRES ::=	am I is I has
V-PAST ::=	had I left I ran I rang I told I was I went I were I woke
V-EN ::=	been I broken I gone I had I left I told

Other categories are the same except no entries for V-ING, and *immediate* becomes an **adjective** in place of *immediately* as an **adverb**.

Exercise 2.9

be'low	*judge'mental*
inse'cure	*di'spute*
rela'tivity	*'haddock*
po'lice	*soli'darity*

Exercise 2.10

There are many such words; two examples are:
   content, present

Chapter 3

Exercise 3.1

John woke to the sound of birds.
nps: birds, John , the sound of birds.

It was the first day of his summer holidays and he was going to stay with his aunt who lived in Devon.

nps: Devon, he, his aunt who lived in Devon, his summer holidays, it, the first day of his summer holidays

Visiting aunts can be fun so he rang the station to discover the times of trains.
nps: aunts, he, the station, the times of trains, trains, visiting aunts

A clerk told him that none of the trains were cancelled but one of them was already full.
nps: a clerk, him, none of the trains, one of them, the trains, them

He decided to leave immediately.
nps: he

He told his mother that he was going and ran to the bus stop.
nps: he, his mother, the bus stop

He passed a train at the station with a broken green locomotive.
nps: a broken green locomotive, a train, he, the station, the station with a broken green locomotive

He boarded the Devon train with his luggage and it left without delay.
nps: delay, he, his luggage, it, the Devon train

John did not know that his aunt had already left her house.
nps: her house, his aunt, John

She was also going on holiday.
nps: holiday, she

Exercise 3.2
See Fig 3.4

Exercise 3.3
he, him, she, them - these cannot appear just anywhere in a sentence. *He* and *she* are **subject pronouns** and can only appear, unqualified, before the main verb. *Him* and *them* are **object pronouns** and can only appear in a noun phrase after the main verb, or in a **rel-cl** after the verb.

Exercise 3.4
(a)   * *a full trains*
Distinguish between singular and plural **determiners** and **nouns**.

(b)   * *a train of she*
Distinguish between subject and object **pronouns**.

Exercise 3.5

e.g.   * *can had is discover*

Exercise 3.6

e.g.   * *John went locomotive.*
          * *His aunt holidays summer.*

Exercise 3.7

Produced:

    Mary cancelled that train.
    Mary saw the grey old grey train.

Not produced:

    John saw Mary.
    The taxi boarded the train.

Exercise 3.8

I	= -poss, -reflex
me	= -poss, -reflex
mine	= +poss, -reflex
myself	= -poss, +reflex
we	= -poss, -reflex
us	= -poss, -reflex
ourselves	= -poss, +reflex
themselves	= -poss, +reflex
their	= +poss, -reflex

Exercise 3.9

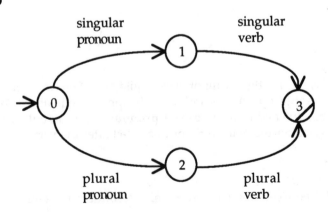

Exercise 3.10

Where VERB is a second person present tense verb form, which also corresponds to an infinitive form, this rule works:

NP1 - VERB - NP2 => 'Do' - NP1 - VERB - NP2 ?

Where VERB is a third person singular present tense form, e.g. goes, we need:

NP1 - VERB - NP2 ==> 'Does' - NP1 - V-INF - NP2 ?

Chapter 4

Exercise 4.1

Rule 16	(**VERB** = *woke*, **POST-VERB** = *to the sound of birds*)
Rule 20	(**PP** = *to the sound of birds*)
Rule 12	(**PREP** = *to*, **NP** = *the sound of birds*)
Rule 6	(**DET** = *the*, **NOUN** = *sound*, **PP** = *of birds*)
Rule 12	(**PREP** = *of*, **NP** = *birds*)
Rule 6	(**NOUN** = *birds*)

Exercise 4.2

4	SIMPLE-NP ::=	PRONOUN |
5		PROPER |
6		[DET] ADJ* CLASF* NOUN PP* [REL-CL] |
7		QU-PH NP
	NP ::=	SIMPLE-NP |
		SIMPLE-NP and NP
15	SIMPLE-VP ::=	[MODAL-PH] [HAVE] BE [ADVB] ADJ |
16		[MODAL-PH] [HAVE] [BE] [ADVB] VERB POST-VERB
	VP ::=	SIMPLE-VP |
		SIMPLE-VP and VP

Exercise 4.3

There are various solutions. One way is to define a new part of speech, **ppn**.

np --> poss_det, adjs, clasfs, noun, ppns, poss_rel_cl.

ppns --> ppn, ppns.
ppns([ ]) --> [ ].

ppn --> prepn, np.
ppn --> pp.

prepn --> [of].   % replaces previous definition

Exercise 4.4

simple_np --> poss_det(Q), adjs, clasfs, noun(Q), pps, poss_rel_cl.

poss_det(Q) --> det(Q).
poss_det(plural) --> [ ].

det(singular) --> [a].
det(singular) --> [the].
det(plural) --> [the].

noun(singular) --> [train].
noun(plural) --> [trains].

Exercise 4.5

simple_vp -->
      poss_modal(T1), poss_have(T1,T2), poss_be(T2,T3),
      poss_adv, verb(T3), post_v.

poss_modal(inf) --> modal.
poss_modal(past) --> [ ].
poss_modal(pres) --> [ ].

poss_have(T1, en) --> have(T1).
poss_have(T,T) --> [ ].

poss_be(T1, past) --> be(T1).
poss_be(T1, ing) --> be(T1).
poss_be(T,T) --> [ ].

verb(T) --> has(T).
verb(T) --> be(T).
verb(inf) --> v_inf.
verb(ing) --> v_ing.
verb(past) --> v_past.
verb(pres) --> v_pres
verb(en) --> v_en.

have(pres) --> [has].
have(inf) --> [have].

have(pres) --> [have].

be(pres) --> [am].
be(inf) --> [be].
be(en) --> [been].
    etc.

Exercise 4.6

See Appendix 1

Exercise 4.7

The existing **post-verb** from 2 to 7 is based on a single **pp** from 2 to 7. Further processing will reveal an alternative **post-verb** from 2 to 7 based on two **pp**s, 2 to 5 and 5 to 7. This will lead to a second **vp** from 1 to 7 and a second **s** from 0 to 7.

Exercise 4.8

start
```
  if  Part-of-Speech = np                     Part_of_Speech = nil
  then   assign_to (Subject, CD-form)         CD_form = nil
         add_to_stack
         ( if  Part_of_Speech = vp
           then assign_to (Concept, CD_form ) )
```
he
```
  if  Part_of_Speech = verb                   Part_of_Speech = np
  then  assign_to (Concept, CD_form )         CD_form = X1
                                              male (X1)
                                              Subject = X1
```

ran
```
  if  Word = to                               Part_of_Speech = verb
  then   add_to_stack                         male (X1)
  ( if  Part_of_Speech = np                   Subject = X1
  then  assign_to (V2, CD_form)               Concept=
   else                                       ptrans( actor=X1,
  if Word = home                              object=X1, to=V2,
   then ( assign_to (V2, CD_form)              from=V3)
      assert (house (CD_form) ) ) )           CD_form=ptrans( actor=X1,
                                              object=X1, to=V2,
                                              from=V3)
```

to

if Part_of_Speech = np
then assign_to (V2, CD_form)

Part_of_Speech = verb
male (X1)
Subject = X1
Concept=ptrans(actor=X1,
  object=X1, to=V2, from=V3)
CD_form=ptrans(actor=X1,
  object=X1, to=V2, from=V3)

the

if Part_of_Speech = noun
then
  assign_to (Part_of_Speech, np)
if Part_of_Speech = np
then assign_to (V2, CD_form)

Part_of_Speech = verb
male (X1)
Subject = X1
Concept=ptrans(actor=X1,
  object=X1, to=V2, from=V3)
CD_form=ptrans(actor=X1,
  object=X1, to=V2, from=V3)

bus stop

Part_of_Speech = np
male (X1)
Subject = X1
Concept=ptrans(actor=X1,
  object=X1, to=bus_stop, from=V3)
CD_form=bus_stop

Result: Concept = ptrans(actor=X1, object=X1, to=bus_stop, from=V3)

Chapter 5

Exercise 5.1

isa(voice, sound).
isa(dog, animal).
isa(aunt, human).
isa(stick, phys).
isa(bang, sound).

vrule(hears, animal, sound).
vrule(carries, animal, phys).
vrule(carries, sound, nil).

Exercise 5.2

A possible hierarchy would be:

```
OBJECTS
  PHYSOBJ              bus | can | house | locomotive | luggage | train
    ANIMATE
      HUMAN            aunt | clerk | John | mother
      NON-HUMAN  bird
  ABSTRACT
      TIME             day | delay | holiday | summer | time
      LOCATION         Devon | left | station

EVENTS
  GO                   arrive | go | leave | run | stay | stop
  EXIST                be | live
  HAVE                 have
  SPEAK                ring | tell
  MENTAL               cancel | decide | discover | know | wake
```

Exercise 5.3

```
SENTENCE             ::= PERSON SPEAK PERSON MESSAGE
MESSAGE              ::= to GENERAL-VP | that GENERAL-S
SPEAK                ::= rang | told
PERSON               ::= PERSON-PRONOUN | PERSON-DESC
PERSON-PRONOUN  ::= he | him
PERSON-DESC          ::= DET PERSON-NOUN
DET                  ::= a | his | the
PERSON-NOUN          ::= clerk | mother | station
```

Exercise 5.4

scase(tell, [subj = yes, iobj = maybe, dobj = yes]).
dcase(tell, [agent = maybe, theme = yes, instrument = maybe,
             goal = maybe, location = maybe]).

vp(tell) --> [told].

The letter told the man that he was resigning.
The man was told that he was resigning by John by letter from home.

Exercise 5.5

```
(forall(X) : (train(X) -> not(cancelled(X))))
   & (exists(Y) : train(Y) & full(Y))
```

s(P) --> simple_s(P).
s(P1 & P2) --> simple_s(P1), conj, s(P2).
simple_s(P) --> np(X, VP, P), vp(X, VP)
quant(X, NNP, VP, forall(X) : (NNP -> not(VP))) --> [none].
conj --> [but].
adj(X, cancelled(X)) --> [cancelled].

Chapter 6

Exercise 6.1

John is the primary actor in the story.

Exercise 6.2

John was moving from London to Devon. He was driving his car there but had no room in it for his luggage. Before leaving London he saw *the Devon train with his luggage* leave from the station.

Exercise 6.3

her house refers to the Home of host, the final location of the event sequence in the OUTWARD_JOURNEY script.

Assumptions: when you go to stay with a person the location is her home, and her house is her home.

Similar story: John's aunt owns a house which she rents out. She lives in a nursing home. She regularly has members of her family to stay with her in a hotel for a holiday.

Exercise 6.4

A: Good afternoon, I want to buy a house.
B: What kind of house are you looking for?
A: Three bedrooms, garage, ..
B: A large garage?
A: Yes, preferably with a workshop.
B: Does it need plumbing and power?
A: Yes.
B: Does it have to have a large garden?

Exercise 6.5
　beginning:　　*by the way,...*
　　　　　　　　incidentally ......

　end:　　　　 *as I was saying* ......
　　　　　　　　to return to the point ....

Exercise 6.6
　QUANTITY (if a train were derailed, the porter should consider this part of
　the requested information).

Chapter 7

Exercise 7.1
　Registers required are:
　　　　verb-tense = { present, past }
　　　　verb-person = { first, second, third }
　　　　verb-qty = { singular, plural }

Exercise 7.2
　We push the **np** network and set the subject register (SUBJ) equal to the
　structure that has been built by the **np** network. When we process the
　AUX arc we output the AUX and then output the contents of SUBJ. (Note
　that nothing is output (*) in the **np** network.)

Exercise 7.3
　The transformational rule is an insertion of *not* between the auxiliary and
　the main verb.

Exercise 7.4
　Use the network solution from Exercise 7.2 and the transformational rule
　from Exercise 7.3.

Exercise 7.5
　A solution to this exercise can be constructed from the solution to Exercises
　7.2, 7.3 and 7.4

Exercise 7.6
　Briefly,　　What is (a) X ?　　　　　　search for: isa(X, Answer)
　　　　　　　(Note: this may require searching a hierarchy of *isa* links)
　　　　　　　Where is (a) X?　search for: location(X, Answer).

Exercise 7.7

To refer to previously named objects:
(a) preceding this reference in the same sentence,
(b) in previous sentence(s) with no intervening object of the same type,
(c) major focus of dialogue.

Exercise 7.8

Rush hour	= busy
running late	= delayed
BR spokesperson	= representative
due to circumstances beyond their control	= unavoidable
The Opposition	= politicians
travelling public	= travellers
paying the price	= suffering because
classic underinvestment in public services.	= low funding

Exercise 7.9

John can pick the apples implies he is physically able to do so.
John may pick the apples implies that he has permission to do so.

Exercise 7.10

[Clause Indicative Declarative Mental Active Explicit]
for *John likes Aunt Betty.*

The wh-question system would contain:
+ Quest > Modal
Quest / Wh
(where Wh is the category name for When, Where, Who, etc.)

This works for most cases. An example to try:

[Clause Indicative Interrogative Wh Action Active]
for *Where may John go?*

Appendix 1

This version of the grammar is reasonably sophisticated. It does not allow too many strange parsings. It expects the story to be in text form in a file called 'book.dat' (the sentences should start with lower case letters). It can be run by simply typing 'go'. Sample output is in Appendix 2.

```
go :- (retract(endtext) ; true),
        see('book.dat'), seen, see('book.dat'),
        repeat,
        (( getsent(Sent), wrlist(Sent), nl,
            phrase(s(PTree),Sent),
            nl, writeTree(PTree), nl, nl);
            true),
        endtext.

s(S) --> simple_s(S).
s(s(S1, C, S2)) --> simple_s(S1), conj(C), s(S2).

simple_s(s(N, V)) --> np(N), vp(V).
simple_s(s(T, V)) --> nvp(T), vp(V).

np(N) --> simple_np(N).
np(np(N1, conj = and, N2)) --> simple_np(N1), [and], np(N2).

simple_np(np(P)) --> pronoun(P).
simple_np(np(P)) --> proper(P).
simple_np(np(D, A, C, H, P, R)) -->
        poss_det(D), adjs(A),
        clasfs(C), noun(H), ppns(P), poss_rel_cl(R).
simple_np(np(Q, N)) --> quph(Q), np(N).
```

```
poss_det(D) --> det(D).
poss_det([]) --> [].

adjs([A | X]) --> adj(A), adjs(X).
adjs([]) --> [].

clasfs([C | X]) --> clasf(C), clasfs(X).
clasfs([]) --> [].

clasf(clasf(N)) --> noun(N).
clasf(clasf(P)) --> proper(P).

ppns([PP | X]) --> ppn(PP), ppns(X).
ppns([]) --> [].

ppn(pp(P, N)) --> prepn(P), np(N).
ppn(pp(P, N)) --> prep(P), np(N).

poss_rel_cl(R) --> rel_cl(R).
poss_rel_cl([]) --> [].

rel_cl(rel_cl(R, V)) --> rel_pron(R), vp(V).

quph(quph(N, (of = of))) --> quant(N), [of].

nvp(nvp(V, P)) --> verb(V, ing), post_verb(P).

vp(V) --> simple_vp(V).
vp(v(V1, conj = and, V2)) --> simple_vp(V1), [and], vp(V2).

simple_vp(vp(M, H, B, ADV, A)) -->   poss_modal(M, T1),
     poss_have(H, T1, T2), be(B, T2), poss_adv(ADV), adj(A), !.
simple_vp(vp(M, H, B, A, V, P)) --> poss_modal(M, T1),
     poss_have(H, T1, T2), poss_be(B, T2, T3), poss_adv(A),
     verb(V, T3), post_verb(P).

poss_modal(M, inf) --> modal(M).
poss_modal(modal = (M, not), inf) --> modal(modal = M), [not].
poss_modal([], past) --> [].
poss_modal([], pres) --> [].

poss_have(H, inf, stop) --> have(H, inf).
poss_have(H, T, en) --> have(H, T).
poss_have([], T, T) --> [].
```

poss_be(B, inf, stop) --> be(B, inf).
poss_be(B, T, ing) --> be(B, T).
poss_be(B, T, past) --> be(B, T).
poss_be([], T, T) --> [].

poss_adv(A) --> adv(A).
poss_adv([]) --> [].

post_verb(post_v(N, A, P, V)) -->
    poss_adv(A), poss_np(N), pps(P), poss_v_mod(V).

poss_np(N) --> np(N).
poss_np([]) --> [].

poss_v_mod(v_mod(T)) --> to_ph(T).
poss_v_mod(v_mod(T)) --> that_ph(T).
poss_v_mod([]) --> [].

pps([PP I X]) --> pp(PP), pps(X).
pps([]) --> [].

pp(pp(P, N)) --> prep(P), np(N).

to_ph(to_ph(inf = to, V, P)) --> [to], verb(V, inf), post_verb(P).

that_ph(that_ph((rel_pron = that),S)) --> [that], s(S).

adj(adj = A) --> verb(v_en = A, en), !.
adj(adj = A) --> verb(v_ing = A, ing), !.
adj(adj = X) --> [X], {dict(adj, D), member(X, D) }.

have(have = X, T) --> [X], {dict(have, D), member(X/T, D) }.

be(be = X, T) --> [X], {dict(be, D), member(X/T, D) }.

verb(v_inf = X, inf) --> [X], {dict(v_inf, D), member(X, D) }.
verb(v_past = X, past) --> [X], {dict(v_past, D), member(X, D) }.
verb(v_pres = X, pres) --> [X], {dict(v_pres, D), member(X, D) }.
verb(v_ing = X, ing) --> [X], {dict(v_ing, D), member(X, D) }.
verb(v_en = X, en) --> [X], {dict(v_en, D), member(X, D) }.

det(det = X) --> [X], {dict(det, D), member(X, D) }.
quant(quant = X) --> [X], {dict(quant, D), member(X, D) }.
noun(noun = X) --> [X], {dict(noun, D), member(X, D) }.
proper(proper = X) --> [X], {dict(proper, D), member(X, D) }.
pronoun(pronoun = X) --> [X], {dict(pronoun, D), member(X, D) }.
prep(prep = X) --> [X], {dict(prep, D), member(X, D) }.
prepn(prepn = X) --> [X], {dict(prepn, D), member(X, D) }.
rel_pron(rel_pron = X) --> [X], {dict(rel_pron, D), member(X, D) }.
modal(modal = X) --> [X], {dict(modal, D), member(X, D) }.
conj(conj = X) --> [X], {dict(conj, D), member(X, D) }.
adv(adv = X) --> [X], {dict(adv, D), member(X, D) }.

% Dictionary

dict(det, [a, her, his, one, the]).

dict(quant, [one, none]).

dict(adj, [first, full, fun, green]).

dict(noun, [aunt, aunts, birds, bus, can, clerk, day, delay,
        fun, holiday, holidays, house, left, locomotive, luggage,
        mother, saw, sound, station, stop, summer, times, train, trains]).

dict(proper, ['Devon', 'John']).

dict(pronoun, [he, him, it, she, them]).

dict(prep, [at, in, on, to, with, without]).

dict(prepn, [of]).

dict(rel_pron, [that, who]).

dict(conj, [and, but, so]).

dict(modal, [can, did]).

dict(have, [had/past, has/inf, have/pres]).

dict(be, [am/pres, be/inf, been/en, is/pres, was/past, were/past]).

dict(v_inf, [be, delay, discover, have, holiday, house, know, leave, mother, sound, station, stay, stop, train]).

dict(v_pres, [am, delay, discover, has, have, holiday, holidays, house, is, know, leave, mother, sound, station, stay, stop, train, trains]).

dict(v_past, [boarded, cancelled, decided, had, left, lived, ran, rang, saw, told, was, were, woke]).

dict(v_en, [been, boarded, broken, cancelled, decided, had, left, lived, told]).

dict(v_ing, [being, going, having, visiting]).

dict(adv, [already, also, immediately]).

% useful routines

```
member(X, [X | _]) :- !.
member(X, [_ | L]) :- member(X, L).
```

% getsent gets the next sentence in list format

```
getsent(WL) :- get0(Ch), getrest(Ch, WL).
```

```
getrest(26, []) :- !, assert(endtext).        % end of file
getrest(46, []) :- !.                          % full-stop = end of sentence
getrest(10, WL) :- !, getsent(WL).             % ignore newline

getrest(32, WL) :- !, getsent(WL).             % ignore spaces
getrest(L, [W | WL]) :-
     getletters(L, Ls, Next),
     name(W, Ls),
     getrest(Next, WL).
```

```
getletters(10, [], 10) :- !.                   % newline
getletters(26, [], 26) :- !.                   % end-of-file
getletters(46, [], 46) :- !.                   % full stop
getletters(44, [], 44) :- !.                   % comma
getletters(32, [], 32) :- !.                   % space
```

```
getletters(L, [L | Ls], Next) :-
    get0(Ch),
    getletters(Ch, Ls, Next).
```

% wrlist writes a list with a space between each pair of elements

```
wrlist([]) :- !.
wrlist([X | Y]) :- write(X), write(' '), wrlist(Y).
```

% wrtree writes out a tree, using bracketing to indicate structure

```
writeTree(=(A, B)) :- !, write(A), write('='), write(B).
writeTree(.(A, B)) :- !, writeList([A, B]).
writeTree(v_mod([], [])) :- !.
writeTree(P) :- P =..[H | T],
        write(' '), write(H), write('('),
        writeList(T), write(')').

writeList([]) :- !.
writeList([[] | T]) :- !, writeList(T).
writeList([H | T]) :- atom(H), !,
        write(H),
        (T=[] ; write(', ')), !,
        writeList(T).
writeList([H | T]) :- writeTree(H),
        (T=[] ; write(' ')), !,
      writeList(T).
```

Appendix 2

What follows is the result of running the program in Appendix 1 against the twelve sentences in the story.

?- go.

John woke to the sound of birds

s(np(proper=John) vp(v_past=woke post_v(pp(prep=to np(det=the noun=sound pp(prepn=of np(noun=birds)))))))

it was the first day of his summer holidays and he was going to stay with his aunt who lived in Devon

s(s(np(pronoun=it) vp(v_past=was post_v(np(det=the adj=first noun=day pp(prepn=of np(det=his clasf(noun=summer) noun=holidays)))))) conj=and s(np(pronoun=he) vp(be=was v_ing=going post_v(v_mod (to_ph(inf=to v_inf=stay post_v(pp(prep=with np(det=his noun=aunt rel_cl(rel_pron=who vp(v_past=lived post_v(pp(prep=in np (proper=Devon))))))))))))))

s(s(np(pronoun=it) vp(v_past=was post_v(np(det=the adj=first noun=day pp(prepn=of np(det=his clasf(noun=summer) noun=holidays)))))) conj=and s(np(pronoun=he) vp(be=was v_ing=going post_v(v_mod (to_ph(inf=to v_inf=stay post_v(pp(prep=with np(det=his noun=aunt rel_cl(rel_pron=who vp(v_past=lived post_v())))) pp(prep=in np ((proper=Devon)))))))))

visiting aunts can be fun so he rang the station to discover the times
   of trains

s(s(np(adj=visiting noun=aunts) vp(modal=can be=be adj=fun)) conj=so s(
   np(pronoun=he) vp(v_past=rang post_v(np(det=the noun=station)
   v_mod(to_ph(inf=to v_inf=discover post_v(np(det=the noun=times
   pp(prepn=of np(noun=trains))))))))))

s(s(nvp(v_ing=visiting post_v(np(noun=aunts))) vp(modal=can be=be
   adj=fun)) conj=so s(np(pronoun=he) vp(v_past=rang post_v(
   np(det=the noun=station) v_mod(to_ph(inf=to v_inf=discover
   post_v(np(det=the noun=times pp(prepn=of np(noun=trains))))))))))

a clerk told him that none of the trains were cancelled but one of them
   was already full

s(np(det=a noun=clerk) vp(v_past=told post_v(np(pronoun=him) v_mod
   (that_ph(rel_pron=that s(s(np(quph(quant=none of=of) np(det=the
   noun=trains)) vp(be=were adj=cancelled)) conj=but s(np (quph
   (quant=one of=of) np(pronoun=them)) vp(be=was adv=already
   adj=full)))))))))

s(s(np(det=a noun=clerk) vp(v_past=told post_v(np(pronoun=him)
   v_mod (that_ph (rel_pron=that s(np(quph (quant=none of=of)
   np(det=the noun=trains)) vp(be=were adj=cancelled))))))) conj=but s (
   np (quph (quant=one of=of) np(pronoun=them)) vp(be=was
   adv=already adj=full)))

he decided to leave immediately

s(np(pronoun=he) vp(v_past=decided post_v(v_mod(to_ph(inf=to
   v_inf=leave post_v(adv=immediately))))))

he told his mother that he was going and ran to the bus stop

s(np(pronoun=he) vp(v_past=told post_v(np(det=his noun=mother)
   v_mod (that_ph(rel_pron=that s(np(pronoun=he) v(vp(be=was
   adj=going) conj=and vp(v_past=ran post_v(pp(prep=to np(det=the
   clasf(noun=bus) noun=stop)))))))))))

s(np(pronoun=he) v(vp(v_past=told post_v(np(det=his noun=mother)
v_mod(that_ph(rel_pron=that s(np(pronoun=he) vp(be=was
adj=going)))))) conj=and vp(v_past=ran post_v(pp(prep=to
np(det=the clasf(noun=bus) noun=stop))))))

he saw one train at the station with a broken green locomotive

s(np(pronoun=he) vp(v_past=saw post_v(np(det=one noun=train
pp(prep=at np(det=the noun=station pp(prep=with np(det=a
adj=broken adj=green noun=locomotive)))))))))

s(np(pronoun=he) vp(v_past=saw post_v(np(det=one noun=train
pp(prep=at np(det=the noun=station)) pp(prep=with np(det=a
adj=broken adj=green noun=locomotive)))))))

s(np(pronoun=he) vp(v_past=saw post_v(np(det=one noun=train
pp(prep=at np(det=the noun=station))) pp(prep=with np(det=a
adj=broken adj=green noun=locomotive)))))

s(np(pronoun=he) vp(v_past=saw post_v(np(det=one noun=train)
pp(prep=at np(det=the noun=station pp(prep=with np(det=a
adj=broken adj=green noun=locomotive))))))))

s(np(pronoun=he) vp(v_past=saw post_v(np(det=one noun=train)
pp(prep=at np(det=the noun=station)) pp(prep=with np(det=a
adj=broken adj=green noun=locomotive)))))

he boarded the Devon train with his luggage and it left without delay

s(s(np(pronoun=he) vp(v_past=boarded post_v(np(det=the
clasf(proper=Devon) noun=train pp(prep=with np(det=his
noun=luggage))))))) conj=and s(np(pronoun=it) vp(v_past=left
post_v(pp(prep=without np(noun=delay))))))

s(s(np(pronoun=he) vp(v_past=boarded post_v(np(det=the
clasf(proper=Devon) noun=train) pp(prep=with np(det=his
noun=luggage)))))) conj=and s(np(pronoun=it) vp(v_past=left post_v(
pp(prep=without np(noun=delay))))))

John did not know that his aunt had already left her house

s(np(proper=John) vp(modal=did, not v_inf=know post_v(v_mod(
that_ph(rel_pron=that s(np(det=his noun=aunt) vp(have=had
adv=already v_en=left post_v(np(det=her noun=house))))))))))

she was also going on holiday

s(np(pronoun=she) vp(be=was adv=also v_ing=going post_v(pp(prep=on
np(noun=holiday)))))

Appendix 3

Prolog code for a very simple case grammar:

```
scase(wake, [subj = yes, dobj = maybe]).
dcase(wake, [theme = yes, agent = maybe]).

s(Deep_Cases) -->
    np(Subj), vp(Verb), poss_np(IObj), poss_np(DObj),
    { convert(Subj, Verb, IObj, DObj, Deep_Cases) }.

convert(Subj, Verb, IObj, DObj, Deep_Cases) :-
    scase_agreement(Verb, Subj, IObj, Dobj) ,
    scase_to_dcase(Subj, IObj, DObj, Deep_Cases),
    dcase_agreement(Verb, Deep_Cases).

scase_agreement(Verb, Subj, IObj, Dobj) :-
    scase(Verb,S_Cases),
    agreement([subj = Subj, iobj = IObj, dobj = DObj], S_Cases).

scase_to_dcase(Subj, _, nil, [theme = Subj]) :- !.
scase_to_dcase(Subj, _, DObj, [agent = Subj, theme = DObj]).

dcase_agreement(Verb, Deep_Cases) :-
    dcase(Verb,D_Cases),
    agreement(Deep_Cases, D_Cases).
%   agreement checks that all present cases are permitted and all
%   necessary cases are present
```

```
agreement(C1, C2) :-
    all_permitted(C1, C2),
    all_present(C1, C2).

all_permitted([], _).
all_permitted([C | C1], C2) :- this_permitted(C, C2), all_permitted(C1, C2).

this_permitted(_ = nil, _ ) :- !.
this_permitted(X = _, C2) :-  member(X = _, C2).

all_present(_, []).
all_present(C1, [C | C2]) :- this_present(C1, C), all_present(C1, C2).

this_present(C1, X = yes) :-  !, member(X = Y, C1), Y \= nil.
this_present(_, _).

np(john1) --> [john].
vp(wake) --> [wakes].
poss_np(nil) --> [].
poss_np(X) --> np(X).

member(X,[X | _]).
member(X,[_ | Y]) :- member(X,Y).
```

Bibliography

Akmajian, A. & Heny, F.W. (1979) *An introduction to the principles of transformational syntax.* 4th ed. MIT Press, Cambridge, Mass

Akmajian, A., Demers, R.A. & Harnish, R. M. (1984) *Linguistics.* 2nd ed. MIT Press, Cambridge, Mass

Allen, J. (1983) Recognising intentions for natural language utterances. In: Brady,M. & Berwick,R.C. (eds) *Computational models of discourse.* Chapter 2. MIT Press, Cambridge, Mass

Allen, J. (1988) *Natural language understanding.* Benjamin/Cummings, Menlo Park, California

Appelt, D. (1985) *Planning English sentences.* Cambridge University Press, Cambridge, UK

Barr, A. & Feigenbaum, E.A.(1981) *The handbook of artificial intelligence.* Vol 1. Walter Kaufman, Los Altos, California

Bratko, I. (1990) *Prolog programming for artificial intelligence.* 4th ed. Addison Wesley, Reading, Mass.

Bruce, B. (1975) Case systems for natural language. *Artificial Intelligence* **6** No. 4, 327-360

Chomsky, N. (1957) *Syntactic structures*. Mouton, The Hague

Chomsky, N. (1965) *Aspects of a theory of syntax*. MIT Press, Cambridge, Mass

Chomsky, N. (1981) *Lectures on government and binding*. Foris, Dordrecht

Chomsky, N. (1982) *Some concepts and consequences of the theory of government and binding*. MIT Press, Cambridge, Mass

Chomsky, N. & Halle, M. (1968) *The sound patterns of English*. Harper & Row, New York

Clocksin, W.F. & Mellish, C.S. (1981) *Programming in Prolog*. Springer-Verlag, Berlin

Cohen, P. & Perrault, C.R. (1979) Elements of a plan-based theory of speech acts. *Cognitive Science* **3** No. 3, 177-212.

Davey, A. (1979) *Discourse production*. Edinburgh University Press, Edinburgh

Earley, J. (1970) An efficient context-free parsing algorithm. *Communications of the ACM* **13** No. 2, 94-102

Fillmore, C.J. (1968) The case for case. In Bach, E. & Harms, R.T. (eds.) *Universals in linguistic theory*. Holt, Rinehart & Winston, New York, pp.1-90

Gazdar, G., Klein, E., Pullum, G. & Sag, I. (1985) *Generalized phrase structure grammar*. Blackwell, Oxford

Gazdar, G. & Mellish, C.S. (1989) *Natural language Ppocessing in Prolog*. Addison Wesley, Wokingham, England

Grice, H.P. (1957) Meaning. *The Philosophical Review* **66** No. 3, 377-88

Grice, H.P. (1975) Logic and conversation. In: Davidson, D. & Harman, G. (eds) *The logic of grammar*. Dickenson, Encino & Belmont, California

Grosz, B.J. (1978) Discourse knowledge. In: Walker, D.E. (ed.) *Understanding spoken language*. New York, North Holland

Halliday, M.A.K. & Martin, J. (eds) (1981) *Readings in systemic linguistics.* Batsford Academic, London.

Joshi, A.K., Levy, L.S. & Takanashi, M. (1975) Tree adjunct grammars. *Journal of Computer Systems Science* **10** No. 1

Kaplan, S.J. (1983) Cooperative responses from a portable natural language database query system. In: Brady, M. & Berwick, R.C. (eds) *Computational models of discourse.* MIT Press, Cambridge, Mass

King, M. (1980) *Parsing natural language.* Academic Press, London

Kukich, K. (1983) *Knowledge based report generation: a knowledge engineering approach to natural language generation.* PhD thesis, Information Science Dept, University of Pittsburgh.

Ladefoged, P. (1982) *A course in phonetics.* 2nd ed. Harcourt, Brace, Jovanovich, New York

Lea, W.A. (1980) Prosodic aids to speech recognition. In: Lea, W.A. (ed) *Trends in speech recognition.* Prentice-Hall, New York, Chapter 8

Lewis, D. (1972) General semantics. In: Davidson, D. & Harman, G. (eds) *Semantics for natural language.* Reidel, Dordrecht-Holland

McDonald, D.D. (1987) Natural language generation. In: Shapiro, S.C. (Ed) *Encyclopedia of artificial intelligence.* Wiley, New York, pp 642-655

McKeown, K. (1985) *Text generation.* Cambridge University Press, Cambridge, UK

McTear, M. (1987) *The articulate computer.* Blackwell, Oxford

Marcus,M.P. (1980) *A Theory of Syntactic Recognition for Natural Language.* MIT Press, Cambridge, Mass

Mann, W. & Matthiessen, C. (1985) NIGEL: A systemic grammar for text generation. In: Freedle, R.O. (ed) *Systemic perspectives on Discourse: Selected Theoretical Papers of the Ninth International Systemic Workshop.* Ablex, Norwood, N.J.

Mendelson, E. (1987) *Introduction to mathematical logic.* 3rd ed. Wadsworth, Monterey

Minsky, M. (1975) A framework for representing knowledge. In: Winston,P. (ed) *The psychology of computer vision.* McGraw-Hill, New York, pp.211-277

Montague, R. (1974) *Formal philosophy.* Yale University Press, New Haven

Morley, J.D. (1985) *An introduction to systemic grammar.* MacMillan, London

Parsons, T. (1987) *Voice and speech processing.* McGraw-Hill, New York

Periera, F.C.N. & Warren, D.H.D (1980) Definite clause grammars for language analysis - a survey of the formalism and a comparison with augmented transition networks. *Artificial Intelligence* **13** No. 3, 231-278

Reichman, R. (1985) *Getting computers to talk like you and me: discourse context, focus, and semantics (an ATN model).* MIT Press, Cambridge, Mass

Rolston, D.W. (1988) *Principles of artificial intelligence and expert system development.* McGraw-Hill, New York

Schank, R.C. & Abelson, R.P. (1977) *Scripts, plans, goals, and understanding.* Lawrence Erlbaum, Hillsdale, N.J.

Schank, R.C. & Colby, K.M. (1973) *Computer models of thought and language.* W.H.Freeman, San Fransisco

Schank, R.C. & Riesbeck, C.K. (eds) (1981) *Inside computer understanding, five programs plus miniatures.* Lawrence Erlbaum, Hillsdale, NJ

Searle, J.R. (1975) Indirect speech acts. In: Cole, P. & Morgan, P. (eds) *Syntax and semantics.* Academic Press, New York

Sowa, J.F. (1984) *Conceptual structures: information processing in minds and machines.* Addison Wesley, Reading, Mass

Sparck Jones, K. & Wilks, Y. (eds) (1983) *Automatic natural language parsing.* Ellis Horwood, Chichester

Weizenbaum, J. (1966) ELIZA a computer program for the study of natural language communication between man and machine. *Communications of the ACM* **9** No. 1, 36-44

Wilks, Y.A. (1973)   An artificial intelligence approach to machine translation. In Schank, R.C. & Colby, K.M. (eds) *Computer models of thought and language.* Freeman, San Francisco, pp.114-151

Winograd, T. (1972) *Understanding natural language.* Edinburgh University Press, Edinburgh

Winograd, T. (1983) *Language as a cognitive process.* Vol.1: Syntax. Addison Wesley, Reading, Mass

Witten, I.H. (1982) *Principles of computer speech.* Academic Press, London

Woods, W.A. (1978)   Semantics and Quantification in Natural Language Question Answering. In Yovits, M. (ed) *Advances in Computers.* Vol. 17. pp 2-64. Academic Press, New York

Zeidenberg, M. (1990)   *Neural networks in artificial intelligence.* Ellis Horwood, Chichester

Index